A PICTURE OF POLEGATE

Compiled by Peter Longstaff-Tyrrell.

GOTEHOUSE PUBLISHING CO.
POLEGATE - EAST SUSSEX.

October 2004 - First Edition.

A mid 1980s aerial aspect of central Polegate.
T.R. BECKETT Ltd.

CONTENTS

Origination by Peter Longstaff-Tyrrell.
Type-set in 10/11pt Sabon.
Gote House Publishing Co.
P.O. Box 169, Polegate BN26 6AA, East Sussex UK.

British Library Cataloguing in Publication Data.

AUTHOR'S INTRODUCTION

In local terms I may be an Incomer, but Polegate seems to be that kind of community. Working in Eastbourne for a dozen years Polegate became a stopping-off place to shop or for recreation. When I eventually deemed it to be a worthwhile centre to re-locate the last thing that I intended to get involved with was local history. This was about the time that the old Junior School in School Lane was ebbing out its last throws and personal research and re-generation projects were pre-occupied with matters of military activities around the county.

As time went by curiosity dwelled on the persona of the town, noting the nominal changes around the High Street with a passing interest. There seemed little written out regarding the transition of Polegate from it's early stages to the 20th century, yet there it was out there to research and compile into a worthwhile format.

The single major factor in producing this account has been the generous access to the Harry Hurdle collection of scenes bequeathed by that archivist to the East Sussex Record Office in Lewes. Regarding the acquisition of text material people kept saying ask Vera! Indeed without the input of Vera Hodsoll the process of getting the book out so agreeably would not have happened as and when it has.

Vera has a fascination with local history, having worked all her life in the ESCC Library Service at numerous locations around Sussex her knowledge blossomed with the passing of the years until she was appointed as Branch Librarian at Polegate Library. After handling all those books over the years it is perhaps ironic that she declined to have her name on the cover of this volume.

Sincere gratitude is conveyed to the ladies that currently staff Polegate Library. Their co-operation towards making this document possible has been considerable. Although no attempt has been made to include every location and activity, simply scenes of some properties and events seem to be non-existent unfortunately.

An innovation with local history books is the Urban Archive section detailing local businesses going back over the years - chronicling consumer changes.

Many people have offered accounts for this book, but getting them to write something out has been another matter. No doubt once publication and circulation takes place we envisage a flurry of recollections. However there are limits to pagination and we hope that the on-going archive herewith is generally appreciated by the people of Polegate.

Thanks are extended to the contributors of information, various illustrations and technical skills . . . Penny Barnes, Tony Boniface, Annette Buckley, Maureen Copping, Jeanne Fry, Pamela Fry, Robert Girling, Bill Hill, Vera Hodsoll, Ian James, Patricia Knight, Edith Levett, Maurice F. Levett, Ron Levett, Roy Martin, Roger Matthews, Sam Richardson and Keith Walton.

Peter Longstaff-Tyrrell, October 2004.

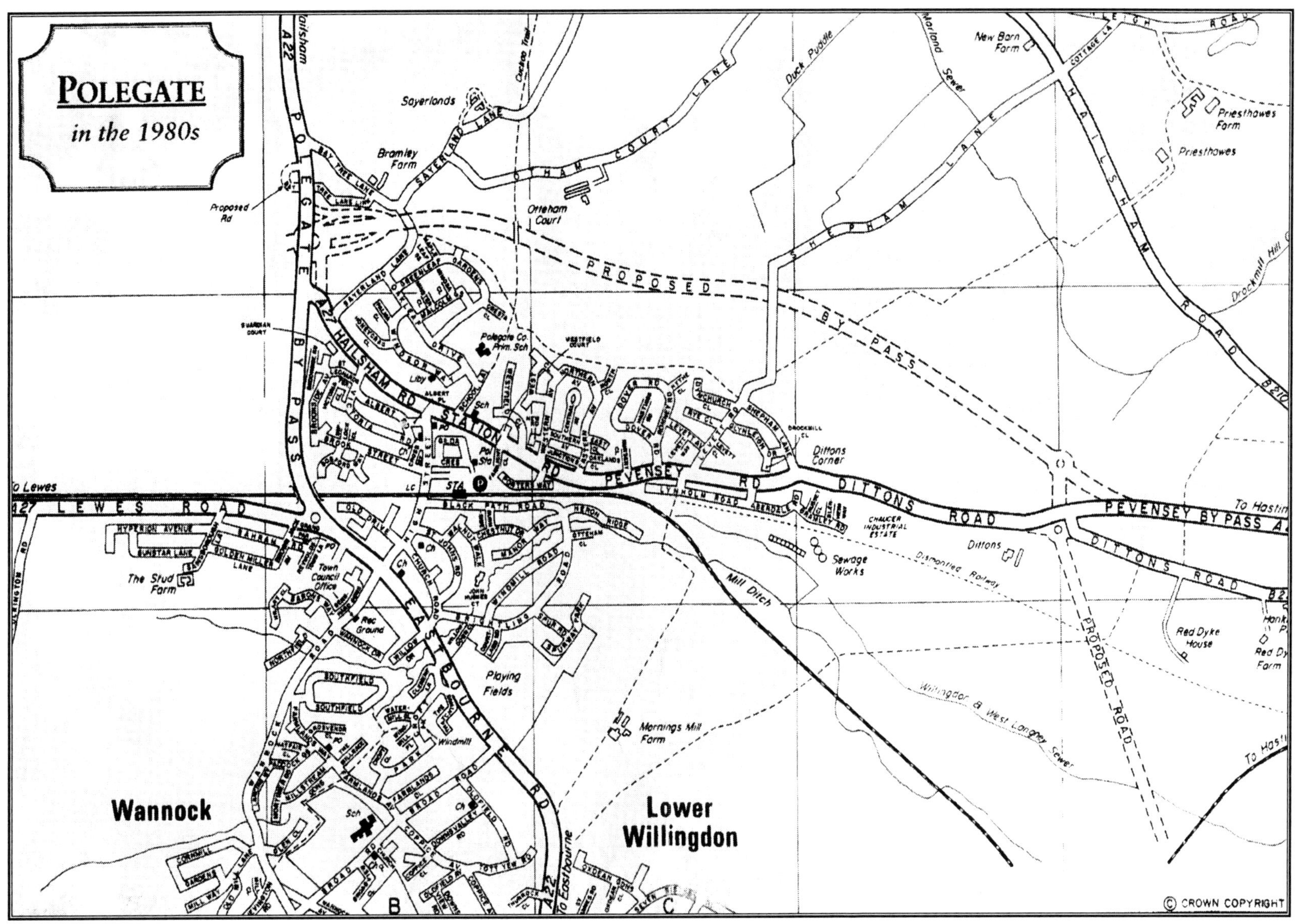

The general layout of the town can be seen in this 1980s aspect relative to the on-going text herein. Note the confusing sequence of road names for the old A27 thoroughfare.

FOREWORD

My concerns for local issues stem from years being away from the district in the RAF, as an airborne radar technician, and a subsequent civilian career invariably absent from home as a radio and television engineer. That subsequent to the early days of Polegate village there was no real long term thought being given to development, other than the apparent build-a-bungalow-a-week type policies. I felt the dire need to establish foundations to hand on the baton as it were. That truly local persons should stake a role in the community. Although, alas, these days invariably younger couples will both be out to work during the day and have shift work or travelling obligations to contend with.

I came with my parents from Hailsham and settled in East Close on the Southlands estate when I was twelve years of age - before taking the King's Shilling as a volunteer for war service. About that age I was encouraged to take banjo lessons from Miss Mabel Lumsden of Eastbourne. One of my greatest regrets was not taking my banjo to war - but that is another story . . .

Now seventy-eight years of age I currently serve on the ESCC representing Polegate district that embraces Laughton, Ripe and Chalvington where I participate in Parish Council activities. On Wealden District Council I am Deputy Chairman of Development Control South. All this as well as being a Polegate Town Councillor and a former Mayor of the community. So my second career is being well and truly fulfilled - serving the community, handing back that baton for future generations.

One vital aspect of the Polegate environs overlooked to date had been a written archive and I more than welcome Peter's account herewith as a memorable, worthwhile and authoritative statement, of Polegate past, present and future.

Councillor Roy Martin, October 2004.

Dedicated to
the people of Polegate.

A PRECIS OF POLEGATE

Vera Hodsoll

The civil parish of Polegate came into being on April 1st 1939. This new parish consisted of 1,677 acres taken from the ancient parishes of Hailsham, Jevington, Westham and Willingdon. Earlier adjustments to the boundaries of those parishes meant that some of their areas had formerly been parts (some detached) of two other parishes - Folkington and Wilmington. However over half of the new Parish of Polegate had been in the south-western corner of Hailsham. Another legal authority with jurisdiction over part of the area for some centuries was the Corporation of the Cinque Port Liberty of Pevensey which lost its powers under the Municipal Corporations Act of 1882.

As Polegate only became a civil parish in 1939 the first census of the civil parish in which it appeared was that of 1951 when the population was 3,564. The Registrar General was able to extract the 1931 figure of 1,618 from the returns of all the parishes which had contributed land area to Polegate. Later census population figures are:- 1961 - 5208, 1971 - 7019, 1981 - 6,794, 1991 - 7,323 and 2001 - 7929.

The name Polegate first appears in records as Powlgate Corner in a 1563 rental of lands formerly held by the Abbey of Bayham, which was in Frant parish on the northern border of Sussex with Kent. Other place names within the present parish are recorded much earlier than this. Lewes Priory held land at Dudintone (around the present main crossroads area) about 1100. Tithes were due to that Priory from . . . thye men of the monks who dwelt there at this time. Around 1115 the Lewes Priory holdings were exchanged with the de Dene family of West Dene for lands elsewhere. It was a later member of that family, Ralph de Dene, who founded Otham as a cell of Premonstratensian Canons around 1185 giving them the nearby lands as an estate for their support. Not caring for the situation the monks sought permission to move and were offered Bayham in Frant where they joined with another church group. Ella de Sackville, the founder's daughter allowed this and confirmed the retention of their holdings in the Polegate area. Otham was let out to farm. However the monks retained the right to lodging and stabling there. Farnestreet, the road to Lewes, is named in the Bayham Abbey records about 1272.

Bayham Abbey was suppressed in 1524 before the general Dissolution of the Monasteries. All its lands were given to Cardinal Wolsey. After his attainder in 1533 the Crown seized the lands and properties and sold them. It is in the estate rentals of these times that the names POLEGATE, SAYERLAND and SWINES appear. The Acton family of Ripe acquired the Manor of Otham. Richard Acton sold 100 acres of the estate to the Fullers, ironmasters of Waldron, in 1692. In the same decade the rest of the holding was sold to Thomas Medley (buried at Buxted in 1728), who had married into a Sussex family and was building up a very considerable estate. These estates eventually descended to the Earl of Liverpool's three daughters in 1851 and from that time sales gradually diminished their local holdings.

The direct, and wealthy, line of Fullers ended with the death of Jack Fuller of Brightling in 1834. His heirs, not resident in Sussex, not even Fuller by name broke the entail, and sold many of their Sussex estates. The steward of the non-resident owners was Frederick Ellman, a solicitor, of Battle. He urged the sale of 100 acres of Swine's Hill Farm at Polegate for development as a new building estate. It is in these documents that the name turns from Swine's to Millfields - a more attractive name perhaps.

THE PARISH AREA

Boundaries using natural features, such as rivers and streams, high points and old trackways, are thought to be amongst the oldest. One here is the stream from Wannock Glen flowing down through Wannock on to Polegate. From its crossing under the road at Wannock it was the Willingdon boundary with the adjoining parishes around and thorough the Willingdon Levels - Jevington, Folkington, Hailsham, and Westham.

TURNPIKE ROADS

The road from Lewes, the county town, to Eastbourne was the subject of a Turnpike Act in 1759. The road came by Willingdon to the top of Polegate High Street where there was a toll house. The road, known as Farnestreet, turned left there along what is now Hailsham Road and continued in a westerly direction through the fields to Selmeston joining another road there. In 1818 a completely new road, (now the A27) on a fresh line was constructed from the southern end of High Street across open farm land to Selmeston. The new Turnpike Act ordained that the old road should be pecked up to prevent its use and thus non-payment of tolls. The toll house at the top of the High Street was sold off and a new one built approximately where the horse-trough stands by the road outside the Horse and Groom.

FARMING

Farming will always have been the major occupations, but it is likely that the area of woodland was greater on the clay lands of the north of the parish. In the 1840s the major farms in the area were Otham, Sayerland, Starvecrow (later known as Nightingale Farm), Cophall and Swine's Hill Farm (later known as Millfields). Although the farmsteads of such farms as Dittons, Priesthawes, Wootton, Folkington, Wannock and others were not in what is now Polegate parish area they had fields here, as did several other more distant farms.

THE RAILWAY

The north-south road from Eastbourne to Hailsham and the east-west road from Pevensey to Lewes crossed at Polegate. The London, Brighton & South Coast Railway, who constructed a line from Brighton to Hastings, opened a station on June 27th 1846. The line crossed some of the Fuller's land, and the station was built where the line crossed the Eastbourne to Hailsham turnpike road in Polegate High Street. Today the railway station is almost on the same spot as then, having moved away only to return to the same site almost a century later.

The railway brought a number of workers here. Others came to find jobs in the immediate area and yet others to cater for their needs. Branch railway lines to Eastbourne and Hailsham opened on May 14th 1849. Only one train shuttled forth and back to Eastbourne and Hailsham. Travellers from those far places had to join trains to Hastings, Brighton and London at Polegate. In 1871 the opening of the loop line from the Polegate to Eastbourne section of the line, near the present day Hampden Park station, did away with the necessity of changing trains for Eastbourne.

In the 1880s the London, Brighton & South Coast Railway completed a line from Hailsham to Tunbridge Wells. So that trains could travel direct from Eastbourne to Tunbridge Wells, without going to the old station at Polegate and backing out, a small section of line was built from the new four platform station about a quarter of a mile further east. After closure of the Tunbridge Wells line the present station was built very close to the site of the original station to replace that in Station Road which has been turned into a public house and restaurant.

The railway purchased enough land to provide an extensive coal and goods yard, with an entrance from High Street. In early days one its functions was as the off loading place for cattle being brought in from Ireland. Here they were sold off to local graziers for fattening up on the nearby marshes and grasslands. There was also a large granary for the storage of cereals. Eastwards of the second station there were numerous sidings, which after WWII became a wagon breaking area.

THE SCHOOLS

The National Society for the Education of the Poor in the Principles of the Established Church (usually known as just The National Society) built a school in Hailsham Road in the 1850s on the instigation of the Vicar of Hailsham, George Gayton Harvey. His father-in-law, the owner of most of Folkington, was also patron of the Hailsham living. The school took children of all ages until the new council school was built in Station Road in 1892. The Infants remained in the old building and those from 7-12 years (the school leaving age) moved into the new school. The Education Act of 1918 put the school leaving age up to 14. Soon after that the children over 11 had to travel to the senior school in Hailsham.

DEVELOPMENT

The first sale of the Fuller lands took place on October 26th 1866. Further sales followed until the remaining plots were sold on May

25th 1877. Some of the plots were sold to be brickyards. Other plots were for large houses and yet others were to be used for the erection of small houses for workers (e.g. Brook Street). Roads were laid out on the estate by Mr W. Beeny, a local coal merchant and brickmaker of Hailsham and Eastbourne. The roads laid out at this time were Church Road, St John's Road (originally named Station Road), Brook Street, Victoria Road and Albert Road. Mr R. Wright of Hellingly bought some of the individual plots for development. The brickyards were situated north of the railway in parts of the parish which had clay soils. The last of the brickyards closed down at the time the first bypass road was built in the mid 1930s.

It was work on one of the brickyards between the main Eastbourne Road and Church Road that brought to light Roman pottery in 1868. Work on the eastern side of High Street near the crossroads continued to turn up more shards over the years. In the 1950s a complete Roman pottery lamp was dug up in St John's Road. Roman coins have been found there and in Victoria Road. It has been suggested that the Roman Road from Pevensey westwards to Lewes ran through the parish - partly along the line of Station Road and the old turnpike route known as Farnestreet. The street element in that name has been offered as evidence for the Roman presence.

THE CHURCHES

A site for a church appeared on the development plan of 1886. The site was given by the owner and building started a decade later. By this time the Vicar of Hailsham was the Rev. Francis Clyde Harvey, son on the Rev. George Gayton Harvey. The church was consecrated on August 6th 1878 as a chapel of ease to Hailsham Parish Church. As Polegate was not a parish local residents who died here were buried at Hailsham either in the churchyard there, or later in the Ersham Road cemetery. Not until 1938 did Polegate become a separate ecclesiastical parish, but we have never opened a cemetery. Ashes after cremation can be placed in the church yard now. The Rev. John C. Salisbury, a curate here since 1933, became the first vicar.

A Congregational Church was established in the High Street, seen on the maps herein, but having joined with others it is now the United Reformed Church. Originally it was set further back, then it was brought forward and later extended backwards. The Roman Catholic Church, St George's, was built at the crossroads on Eastbourne Road in 1938-1939.

A WELL KNOWN RESIDENT

Caleb Diplock, an Eastbourne brewer, wine merchant, mineral water manufacturer and hotel and public-house owner bought land in the corner created by High Street, the Lewes Road and the railway line. Here he built Southdown Hall, the largest house in Polegate in the 1870s. His son, Caleb Diplock, the younger, died unmarried in 1936. He made a will making some bequests, but the majority of his property was to be sold and given to charitable causes chosen by his executors. The house was demolished, and the grounds became the site for housing. Only half a dozen, or so, were built before the start of WWII.

Some construction material was salvaged from Southdown Hall and incorporated into the first houses to go up. Wannock Coppice, renamed Diplock's Wood, and the Diplock Cottage Homes are reminders of young Caleb's will legacy. As he had requested that most of his assets should go to good causes his solicitors had carried out his wishes. A claim to have the will declared invalid was made by several kinsmen and in due course accepted. All the money spent or distributed had to be returned for the claimants. Diplock's Wood, which had been presented to the people of Polegate, was bought by Hailsham District Council. There was then an attempt to call it Rowland Gwynne Wood - he at that time being the Rural District Council Chairman. The Cottage Homes were purchased by the Quakers with money donated by Bernhard Baron, a tobacco millionaire.

MILLS

When part of the Parish of Willingdon was transferred to the new Parish of Polegate in 1939 it brought both the Windmill (built in 1817) and the watermill (built in 1833) into Polegate, they being part of Willingdon parish south of the Wannock Mill Stream which was brought into the new parish. There had been windmills in Polegate previously. In digging out foundations for new flats in School Lane parts of two wooden centre-posts were excavated. It is thought the better one (which was transferred to the windmill for preservation and storage) may be of 15th century origin. There is an early mention of the Abbot of Bayham's mill.

OTHER BUSINESSES

Three public houses (or beer houses) set up in business - The Horse & Groom, The Polegate Inn (now known as The Dinkum) and the Junction Hotel - this last after the coming of the railway. Both the present Horse & Groom and The Junction are not on their original sites. When the original station moved a new Junction Hotel was built opposite the second station. The old building was sold to the railway company and used as housing by signalmen and level crossing gatekeepers, now it is a small car park. When the 1930s Polegate bypass was built a new Horse & Groom was erected at the north-west corner of the crossroads. The old building was used by local groups and Civil Defence until it was replaced by a garage after WWII. The Thoroughbred was created postwar by amalgamating two Grand Parade properties.

There seems to have been a blacksmith in the High Street for many years. He would have been an essential worker throughout the centuries. In its latter days it was workshops and taxi garage with a petrol pump. Soon after the first land sales we find two rows of shops in High Street with accommodation over. That nearer the railway station has a back alleyway - Cross Street.

Over the years there have been several nurseries and numerous laundries. Two nurseries were situated in the Church Road/St John's Road area. Others came and went over the years in Brook Street, Hailsham Road, Station Road and Pevensey Road. The laundries were situated off Victoria Road and in High Street. Mertonville at the top of the High Street advertised that is used soft water and kept twenty irons working.

James Tolhurst, a baker and confectioner, came to Polegate about 1870. Later he concentrated on making sweets. He and his successors continued in business for over a century and latterly moved in to new premises after WWII on the Chaucer Industrial Estate on the eastern edge of the parish off Dittons Road.

HOUSING DEVELOPMENT

The Compton and Cavendish (Dukes of Devonshire) families owned much land in this area, including farms in Jevington, Westham and Willingdon. Horse racing stables were established in Jevington in the latter half of the 1800s. When the 7th Duke was succeeded in 1891 by his son as 8th Duke the latter set up a new stud south of the A27 road towards Folkington. After his death the stud was was acquired by Solly Joel, a diamond mine owner and horse breeder, for a period.

The Stud Farm house is still there - the entrance is in now Gainsborough Lane. The Mile Oak Estate developers gave all the roads there names of famous racehorses, but none were named after those who had trained there. Sunstar won the 1911 Coronation Derby. Grand Parade won the 1929 Derby. Golden Miller won the Grand National in 1934, Hyperion the St Leger and Derby in 1933. Bahram won the 1936 St Leger. Reynoldstown won the 1935 Grand National and Brown Jack won the Ascot in 1927/1928.

In 1935 the 230 home Stud Farm estate was developed - six bungalows to the acre, with the ESCC stipulation that the 100 foot wide coppice parallel to the A27 would remain as an area of land known as The Lawns. Adverts described the estate as styled on a model garden city. Bungalows were priced from £550 and unusually as freehold in this area.

One feature of the estate was the installation of electric heating and fittings. In 1942 the first allotment show was held and over the years annual gatherings have taken place on the allotments plot in Hyperion Avenue.

With the passage of time the developers name has been largely forgotten and the estate is known as the Stud Farm Estate. Originally local people called the estate the green roof estate, as all the roofs, and most of the window frames, were green in colour.

Not until after WWI was there any large scale development. The 1930s saw the building of the Stud Farm Estate, Southlands Estate, Old Drive, Brightling Road and Gilda Crescent with the shops either side of its entry in High Street.

BREAKING UP THE FULLER ESTATES

John Fuller, known as Honest Jack or Mad Jack, of Rose Hill, Brightling, died unmarried on April 11th 1834. He was succeeded by Augustus Eliott Fuller, the eldest son of his first cousin, John Trayton Fuller (died 1811). Augustus Eliott Fuller on succeeding made moves to end the entail on the estates. The document validating this was signed October18th/20th 1834. He died on August 5th 1857, and his will was proved October 29th 1857.

He had married Clara Meyrick, eldest daughter and heiress of Owen Putland Meyrick, of Anglesey, where the family had been established since the time of Henry VIII. The only son of Augustus Eliott Fuller, Owen John Augustus Fuller had assumed the additional surname Meyrick in 1825 and in 1856, before his father's death, was resident on the Meyrick estates at Bodorgan, Anglesey.

It was Owen John Augustus Fuller Meyrick who put into motion the sale of Swine's Hill Farm in Hailsham, which had been created during the Fuller's possession since 1692. To be able to create freeholds the copyhold rights then in the possession of Reginald Bray of Shere, near Guildford, Surrey were released to O.J.A.P. Meyrick for the sum of £106.13.4 on September 27th 1866. Being described as . . . the Pound Fields, Cherry Croft and Cow Fields, but now known by the general name of Swine's Hill Farm in the occupation of Richard Lamb and containing the whole by estimation 100acres (more or less) being formerly part of the desmesne land of the Manor of Otham . . . in the Parish of Hailsham in the said county of Sussex.

A valuation on October 23rd 1866 paid Richard Lamb £149.12.2d for his work and loss of crops on his land. The first auction of plots took place at the Anchor Hotel, Eastbourne, on October 26th 1866.

O.J.A.F. Meyrick died unmarried on February 12th 1876, and his will was proved March 9th 1876. The surviving son and daughter of his only sister, Clara (d. 1831), the wife of Sir George William Tapps-Gervis (d. 1842), and his great niece, daughter of their deceased brother succeeded to the estates.

Sir George Eliott Meyrick Tapps-Gervis formerly added Meyrick to his surname after his uncle's death. Whilst he received the estates his sister, Clara (d. unmarried 1910) and their niece, Augusta Maria, were to receive cash sums of £10,000 and £8,000 respectively.

The will specified that this was to come from the sale of Ashdown, East Grinstead (now in Forest Row parish), and other estates. Clara Tapps-Gervis gave her consent to the sale of the remaining 61 acres of the Polegate estate on August 2nd 1876. She may have taken Ashdown at valuation as she is resident there in the directory for 1878. The Brightling estate, including Rose Hill, was sold in 1879.

A proportion of the Polegate land was bought by George Clement of Silverhill, Hastings on May 26th 1877 for £7,537. This price included some properties already erected on the land, Clement Lane is named after him. The land by the mill stream was designated in the original plan to be put to use as a waterworks. This proved not to be needed as the Eastbourne Waterworks Company undertook operations elsewhere.

Sir George Eliott Meyrick Tapps-Gervis-Meyrick was in turn succeeded by three further generations - all father to son, and all Sir George, and the current holder of the baronetcy also a son, George. The family of Gervis has been resident at Christchurch, Hampshire since the 17th century, at least, and the present Baronet has residences at both Hinton Admiral, Christchurch, and Bodorgan, Anglesey.

Until comparatively recently the old family still retained some interest in the Polegate land as their permission had to be obtained when some local people wished to excavate in the playground of the former Infants' School in Hailsham Road in 1972.

Vera Hodsoll.

COMMUNITY DEVELOPMENT

On July 4th 1877 there was a sale by auction at the Diplock Assembly Rooms in Eastbourne of the scheduled Polegate Building Estate. The initial road plan had been laid out and the plots to be auctioned were offered at Victoria Road, Albert Road, Brook Street, Cross Street, and in Hailsham Road some six sites were available including nine plots where Nelson Terrace was built. All this was seen as a model village, with an abundance of trees lining the highways. At the corner of Victoria Road and Hailsham Road a site was allocated for the erection of a hotel, although it did not take place. The original Junction Hotel existed at the time at Black Path beside the level crossing. A site at the end of Brook Street was acquired by a Hastings brewer for an inn, but the site remained vacant for many years until being built over with offices and homes.

Subsequent to this sale Brook Street started to become developed where Mabel Terrace was built at the eastern end in 1880 and by the 1890s there were 17 terraced houses running westward from Cross Street. Most of the homes in Victoria Road and Albert Road were 1920s-1930s built, followed by the creation of Stud Farm, Southlands and Brightling Road estates. The council estates at Northfield off Wannock Road and Park Croft date from the 1950s, with Southfields being a last expansion.

Builders taking the early opportunity to develop the community were Stephen Message and James Tolhurst. Stephen Message built Mabel Terrace in Brook Street and St John's Terrace in the High Street amongst others. Most of the homes on the north side of Station Road between the railway bridge and The Junction were erected by James Tolhurst who sought, it is said, to preserve their downland views by acquiring the field opposite.

The lively community spirit in Polegate has been generated from the late 19th century, invariably starting from church organisations. A Working Men's Club was formed in Brook Street in the early 1890s, some 90 members taking part in the Slate Club in 1893. Each paid sixpence weekly which provided 10/- a week sick benefit for eight weeks. Any balance being shared between the participants. Football and cricket clubs came into being, associated to the church and its organisations. That same year the Infants School accommodated a series of Horticultural Lectures provided by the Technical Education Committee. Mr Diplock hosting a Cottage Gardners Show in his Home Field in 1898. Polegate also had a popular Fife and Drum Band, Bonfire Boys and Handbell Ringers. Invariably these activities were led by Mr Cornelius Taylor who arranged functions and church excursions into the neighbouring villages. In mid 1906 the fife section was replaced by bugles and all fourteen buglers and four drummers marched to Willingdon and back.

In the early 1900s the Working Men's Club moved to 8 High Street in a room above the then Davy's Tea Shop. Then in 1906 Mr Diplock, a keen supporter of their activities, established new premises for them in Brook Street. Rev. Stuart Fox also had a keen interest in the working men's welfare, managing to average 75 of them at his Men's Services. In January 1907 some 164 men were at St John's escorting a brass band from Hankham to the church.

In 1901 it was proposed to create a Church Hall in the grounds of St John's, partially to commemorate Queen Victoria and also the turn of the century. Funds for the Victoria Memorial Church Room and Recreation Room were generated and a freehold plot was found at the corner of Cross Street and Victoria Road with a token rental for 21 years. The single storey hall being opened in 1907.

The Congregational Church and Mission Room in the High Street dates from this period, a brick church being built on the site in 1904 and became the United Reformed Church after WWII. St John's built their new hall alongside their church in 1960 and the the United Reformed Church took over the Victoria Road meeting place that continues to serve a variety of community needs.

Vera Hodsoll.

THE GROWING TOWN

In 1959 the only premises in Polegate able to seat 100 people were St John's (now Free Church Hall) and the Junction Hotel, whilst the village Young People's Club found a home in the Tudor Cafe (Thoroughbred Inn) run by Geoffrey Maynard. New estates were pushing the population up to 8,000 people, with an influx of residents demanding better facilities. A spree of fund raising followed and the sum of £24,000 was achieved. On May 10th 1969 the new Community Centre was opened in Windsor Way.

Such is the degree of social life in Polegate that a larger floor space was gradually required. This demand escalated and during 1975 an extension to house the Windsor Club room and Activity Room were built on the original car park plot at a cost of £27,000. A further extension was made to the main hall which involved a larger stage, with extra storage space and included a dressing room/committee room that were completed in 1982 at a cost of £42,500.

The present Community Centre was considered to be the finest of its kind in East Sussex and became the flagship of the East Sussex Federation of Community Centres. The range of activities embraces every age group, from playgroups through to vibrant senior citizens club.

The strengths lie in its membership of almost 2,000 people, in nine active sections ranging from badminton, sequence dancing, short mat bowls, table tennis, its fund-raising sections, bustling social section, the drama group, plus the licensed Windsor Club. Strong management committees ensure that there is no drain on public funding back-up the infrastructure of the facilities enjoyed by almost fifty affiliated groups.

The land on which the Community Centre was built had been leased and in 1998 the freehold was acquired for the sum of £5,000, this sum being met by a bequest from the will of Mrs C.A. Wills. The association continues to flourish via occasional donations, legacies and community projects - making it very much the social centre of the town.

Vera Hodsoll.

SOUTHDOWN HALL - THE DIPLOCKS

Today's Polegate has grown up considerably over the last century and a half. When the railway arrived in 1846 just a few buildings fringed what is now the High Street. Undeveloped farm land stretched unbroken from the village of Willingdon, on it's hilltop, to the small market town of Hailsham. Scattered here and there were farmhouses. In the area now covered by the parish of Polegate were four or so old farmhouses, the two major ones being Otham and Sayerland. When the Fuller family decided to sell their Polegate holding, adjacent to the railway and the roads, one of the selling points was the ease of access to Eastbourne and London by train.

Eastbourne at this time boasted two breweries. These were the old established firms of Robert Cooper in South Street, and Alexander Hurst's Star Brewery in Old Town. Then in the 1850s a newcomer came to the expanding resort as a wine and spirit merchant. Caleb Diplock (1818-1884), a Rotherfield born man and son of a farm worker, had migrated to London in his youth to seek his fortune. There he married a wife, Sarah, and had at least two children who survived.

The expanding resort of Eastbourne raised hopes that business could be good, so the young family moved south. Terminus Road, Eastbourne, was opened in 1851, and to begin with contained some private homes and boarding establishments.

The Diplock's moved in 1856 and started in business. Caleb, senior, began a process of expansion. The Commercial Hotel and the London House, on opposite corners of Pevensey Road, soon became part of the empire. On both sides of the road behind them a new brewery, malt-house, and stores appeared. At the opening of the Lion Brewery in 1863 Caleb, the elder, paid tribute to Caleb, the younger, then only twenty, by saying . . . had it not been for my son, who is of a business habit, neither of these buildings would have been erected. A mineral water manufactuary, wine stores, and public houses followed. Caleb, senior, was elected to the first Local Board in Eastbourne in 1859. He continued to be elected to the Board for the whole of its life until 1883 when it was replaced by the Town Council.

For some unknown reason when the Diplock's chose to build a new house for themselves they chose Polegate, when many of the other business men in Eastbourne were moving into Upperton Road and Meads areas, both of which were expanding. Could the railway have been an influence? However, the Diplocks bought the area of land bounded by the railway, High Street, and the Lewes Road. There they proceeded to build a substantial house, Southdown Hall, into which father, mother and the children moved into during the 1870s. As benefited a wine merchant the ground floor of the house was raised above the surrounding land to provide beneath what the sale brochure later called extensive cellarage. A verandah, on the garden front, approached by steps gave support to climbing plants, and some shade to the principal reception rooms of the house. The handsome drawing room on the south-east corner was 26ft by 20ft, and opening into it was a splendid tiled conservatory 31ft by 19ft.

As well as the drawing room there were rooms almost as large for the dining, breakfast and billiards rooms. Two staircases led up from the tiled central hallway to a galleried landing off of which led six large bedrooms. The two servants bedrooms were up in the attics with the stores, tank room and linen cupboards. The house stood nearer the road than the railway, and between it and the railway trees and shrubs were planted. There were in addition stables, barns and sheds.

Frederick Diplock was born in 1858 at Eastbourne, but died aged 39 years in May 1897. Sarah Matilda, wife of Caleb senior, died aged 62 in January 1881. The following year Caleb married again, this time to a Sarah Susanna, a lady of mature years. However this marriage was not to last as Caleb himself died in 1884. Neither Caleb junior, or sister Sarah, ever married. Together with their stepmother all three lived out the rest of their lives at Southdown Hall, taking an interest in the people and social life of the growing community.

During the last years of the elder Caleb's life the brewery and wine business had been sold, but the younger Caleb who had the gift for business retained some titles to the property, and acquired more, and joined various business ventures. He was a major shareholder in the Eastbourne Gas Company. In Polegate he liked to act the squire, and was generous with his time, and money - when he thought it had been earned. He would lend his Home Field for village events, games and fetes. He sat on many of the local organising committees. At times all did not go his way. There was a time when the local vicar was very much against alcohol, but Caleb would still take an interest in the local Young Crusaders temperance organisation. When National Insurance scheme was introduced he really took the huff and let it be known that as the tax-man was taking money from him for the poor, then they need not come to him directly.

In the early 1900s a new person arrived at Southdown Hall. She was yet another Sarah, born in Brighton 1859, so she was renamed Sophie. Sophie Watkins came to look after the second Mrs Diplock who died in February 1910, but she stayed on as a companion and friend of Sarah and Caleb. Caleb's sister, Sarah, died in 1916, leaving him at 74 years the last surviving member of the immediate family.

In his bereavement Caleb had a new will drawn up the same year. Nearly twenty years later Sophie Watkins, the companion of his old age, died in July 1935 aged 76 years and Caleb himself died in March 1936 aged 95 years. Sophie Watkins shares the same burial plot in Ocklynge with the rest of the family. The will of 1916 had never been altered, so it was brought out and probate was granted. Caleb's business acumen had resulted in a personal fortune of £533,214 - at today's values he would have been a multi-millionaire.

What happened next belongs to the national record books. The will was proved, and the estate distributed. Then distant relatives chose to contest the will on the grounds that parts of it were ambiguous. They eventually won their case and every penny that had been given to charities had to be returned and be distributed to the claimants. The case entered the record books as being the longest running disputed case.

By this time Southdown Hall and its grounds had been sold. The nine acre plot with all the buildings was auctioned in the autumn of 1936. The lot containing the house realised only £3,400 and it was demolished soon afterwards. The houses built in Old Drive before WWII contained some materials rescued from the old house.

How sad that the house built lavishly only sixty years before should have only housed the one family who built it, and that the family's fortune, too, should be lost in such a way. The two lodge houses remain today as reminders of this story, as does the stag standing in the grounds of the Bernhard Baron Cottage Homes. Some of the garden urns bought at the 1936 auction may still be around in Polegate gardens. Southdown Court, built after WWII, just about stands on the the site of Southdown Hall.

Vera Hodsoll.

RELIGION IN POLEGATE

In 1873 a meeting was held at the Horse & Groom attended by Messrs W.A. Raper, in the chair, with R.K. Blessely, B. Bradford, J. Breton, Drewett, Caleb Diplock, Catt, Gladwin both senior and junior, Hartfield, H.F. Hellman, W. Kirkland, A. Hurst, Larkin, E. Mewett, E. Pound, Simmonds, Tolhurst, Waters and Wright with a view to establishing a church in the community.

During 1875 the village of Polegate was under the care of Hailsham Parish Church and with a population of some 500 souls it was decided to create a church locally. Mr Fuller-Meyrick donated a site and offered £500 towards the estimated cost of £2,700 to build the church. The foundation stone of St John's was laid in 1875, the church being built to sit 270 people. Constructed in Kentish rag stone and designed in Early English style the church was completed in 1876. The Venerable Robert Sutton MA, Archdeacon of Pevensey, opened the church on November 10th 1876, he preached St Matthew Ch21 v13 - My house will be called a house of prayer.

St John's was consecrated August 6th 1878 by the Bishop of Chichester. The licence for marriages was granted June 7th 1879 and the first marriage in the register is dated August 24th that year. The church organ was first used on Easter Sunday 1881. The east end window is dedicated to Glory of God in loving memory of C.B.P. Groves who drowned in 1888. The east side stained glass window was provided by Mr Mendel in memory of his wife who died in 1891. He also presented the bookstand at the altar.

Francis Clyde Harvey, Vicar of Hailsham, was appointed to undertake the care of St John's. There was no lighting or heating in the church, the congregation having to take candles to stand by windows, until 1909 when Miss Diplock paid for the installation of mains gas. The Diplock's played a leading role in establishing the church. They provided the east window (with Caleb Diplock portrayed as a disciple), and the ornate reredos. Miss Sophie Diplock passed on in January 1916, leaving a great void in the community.

The Rev. S.F. Ackroyd was the first of fifteen curates, serving between 1876 and 1887. He lived some distance away until Mr Fuller-Meyrick gave an adjoining plot to create a parsonage. The parsonage was finished in 1881 for the sum of £1,285. On January 19th 1879 the first baptism ceremony took place at St John's when Alice Naomi Waters was baptised by Rev. S. Ackroyd. The first wedding there took place between Frederick William Crowhurst and Sarah Elizabeth Standen on August 24th 1879. The first Holy Communion was held January 1888 and the first Confirmation took place on May 3rd 1901. The Rev. Ackroyd's father presented an organ to St John's and St John's congregation initially heard it play on Easter Day 1881 - that organ remains in use to this day.

In 1893 the Rev. Clifford Aston M.A. was appointed Vicar of St John's. Sidesmen were Mr Levett and Mr Daniels, caretaker was George Taylor. Between 1906-1908 the lively Rev. Stuart Fox revived male participation in the congregation, increasing from 76 men to 164 on Sunday afternoons. The church hall in Victoria Road was erected during his time at St John's - now it is owned by the United Reformed Church as their hall. Between 1908-1919 the Rev. Jackson was curate at St John's, before he moved on to become a C.M.S. Missionary in Bengal for fifteen years. Rev. Jackson and his wife were in Switzerland when he was declared. Belgian refugees were billeted in Polegate. The Red Cross under Miss Henderson did valiant work locally. The memorial tablet on St John's north wall of the nave bears the names of fifty-eight Polegate men who fell in the Great War.

Cornelius P. Taylor, known as Corrie Taylor, was a man of many talents who worked for the church from his youth to the end of his life, supported by his wife. Corrie was in the choir, was Sunday School Superintendent, leader of the Young Crusaders with the drum and fife band that paraded through the village. Corrie lived at Craignaish in Church Road. Another man of note was Mr Page, the organist for twenty-three years and never any friction with the clergy or choir. He was a warden and lay reader. Mr G. Thorpe served the church for over fifty years and also did much for the choir. His son W. Thorpe followed in Mr Page's footsteps as organist for thirty years.

The departure of Rev. H. Jackson, Vicar of Hailsham who had borne all the burdens of St John's, started the evolution that was to make Polegate a Parish on October 22nd 1937. The Rev. C. Salisbury, Curate at St John's since 1933, was inducted as Vicar on January 12th 1938. Next the Rev. R.A. Leonard was inducted on May 30th 1940 and remained in the parish after the war when he carried out several major repairs to the fabric of the church.

A new floor had been laid in 1943, the timber coming from Willingdon Hall. The church spire was re-shingled in 1946 and the windows were renewed in 1949. As no stoker could be found to attend the coke boilers Rev. Leonard raised the money to install gas heaters in 1947. The Youth Club raised over £200 to repair the church room after the soldiers left. An electric blower was added to the organ in 1948. In 1951 the Rev. Leonard accepted a living a Westfield, but returned to Polegate to retire. He married Connie Tyhurst, one of his Sunday school teachers, in 1961.

The parish continued to grow. A hut was rented in Lower Willingdon for those who could not get to St John's for services and the primary school was given up in 1949. The Bishop of Lewes inducted Rev. Harry Parsons on February 24th 1951. He took over a lively church, free from debt and well supported in many ways. It was discovered later that year that the roof was in need of repairs. £700 had been contributed. The parish was extended to nine square miles and from the 1873 census of 500 people the community now comprised of 1,500 people. Rev. Parsons was responsible for building the transept, for planning a fine new hall and founding the daughter church of St Wilfrid's at Lower Willingdon.

The choir at St John's first wore surplices in June 1920, and robes were dedicated for use when Mrs Carter was organist and Choir mistress. St John's witnesses its evangelical tradition with interest in the church overseas. Rev. Peter Thompson was appointed to St John's in 1974 after being a missionary in Burma. With a fervent enthusiasm for mission and for St John's he built up the church in this area. He was made a canon and eventually retired in 1992.

The Rev. Canon David Gutsell came to St John's in 1993, and

the church underwent major alterations when the interior was ripped out and refurbished at a cost of £76,000. Church services were held in the adjoining hall from August 1995, until the rededication service on December 3rd 1995. Preacher that day was Rev. Douglas Milmine, formerly the Bishop of Paraguay, followed by a buffet lunch. To end the year a Humpty Dumpty pantomime was performed on December 2nd 1995.

In 1997 St John's held a flower display titled Polegate Places and Pastimes to celebrate the re-start of the Carnival after a break. Church Army Captains help with the youth of the church and a thriving Sunday Club meets every Sunday morning. In 2000 the vicar to succeed David Gutsell was announced as the Rev. Mark Lucas. His inauguration took place on Wednesday September 13th 2000, with the Bishop of Lewes and the Archdeacon of Lewes and Hastings officiating and the Rural Dean leading the service. The Bishop welcomed Polegate MP Norman Baker, the town Mayor and other officials.

ST WILFRID'S CHURCH

After forty years of being the daughter church of St John's on January 1st 2002 St Wilfrid's in Broad Road became established in its own right - having outgrown its parent.

ST GEORGE'S CHURCH

Locally Mass was celebrated at Otham Priory circa 1175 when a chapel was established there dedicated to St Laurence. This was built on the site of an earlier chapel that is now Otham Court which is privately owned.

St George's Church built at the crossroads on Eastbourne Road was opened on Wednesday December 7th 1938. The construction cost was some £4,000, the site cost £1,300 and fittings amounted to £500. Seating for 120 people was allowed for by the architect, who collaborated with the builder who possessed a quantity of Sussex boulders used for the main fabric of the building. The church interior was intended to be austere. Father Peter Tak was the priest in charge Hailsham and Polegate in the Roman Catholic Diocese of Southwark. Arch Bishop Peter Emmanuel Amigo presided over the opening High Mass.

During WWII a priest served St George's from Our Lady of Ransom Church in Eastbourne. In 1958 Father John Flanagan became Parish Priest for Polegate and Hampden Park. At that time the fabric and furnishings at St George's had deteriorated considerably and an appeal for replacements went out. In 1965 they became separate parishes and Father Flanagan moved to live in Polegate. The Hall and Presbytery were built in the early 1960s. In 1965 the Diocese of Southwark was divided. Surrey, East and West Sussex form the Diocese of Arundel and Brighton.

Father Flanagan died in 1977 and he was succeeded by Father James Kenny who became Parish Priest, until ill health caused him to retire after six years. Canon Bernard Thom was the next Parish Priest for some three years. In 2003 because of a shortage of priests there was a re-organisation of the Catholic church. Some time earlier water had been discovered under the building and subsidence occurred which had to be rectified at considerable cost.

In June 2003 Father Tony Shelley took over at St George's Church, having previously been at St Wilfrid's in Hailsham. His Polegate appointment marked his 40th anniversary of service in the priesthood.

UNITED REFORMED CHURCH

Originating back in the late 1860s as a corrugated iron roofed Mission Hall, that seated about fifty people, the town's United Reformed Church underwent an exterior face lift in January 2001. The frontal area received a makeover that included a new canopy and disabled access ramps. At the same time new toilet facilities for disabled worshippers were installed.

The church had previously been extended and modernised in 1981. Addressing over 300 people at a service of Thanksgiving and Dedication Rev. Cyril Franks, Moderator of the Southern Province, gave a challenging address saying the new premises were not an architectural exercise and that they were only a beginning. The minister then was Rev. Fred Moore. Currently the Rev. Reg Spice leads the congregation. *Maureen Copping.*

BOARD SCHOOL AND INFANTS SCHOOL

A new school to meet the demands of the growing population and compulsory education was built alongside Station Road 1893. Known as the Board School it opened on March 5th 1894 and accommodated 166 children, construction cost £2,599. This took juniors and the average attendance was 115 pupils, infants remained at the Hailsham Road premises for some years. Tutors for 1893-1894 at the new school were George Loads, Certified Teacher, H. Gayler, Assistant and Kate Loads, Assistant Art.

In February 1893 the school was issued with slates and framed writing boards for the children to use and in March they received new books and a storage cupboard. On March 3rd 1893 the school was closed for use as a Poling Station. Some of the children admitted that year were Louise Hillier, Fred and Edwin Gates, Louisa and Eva Putland, Edward Morris, Henry Bridge and Percy Ricks. Examined for certificates in 1898 were Clifford Elphick, William Hoather, Leonard Page, George Cottingham, Fred Horn, William Vidler, Annie Carter and Leonard Parsons.

The new school

Opened in 1969 the Oakleaf Drive premises have undergone a sequence of expansion and technical progress. In December 1990 former headmaster Bill Usherwood opened the premises that had been doubled in size at a cost of £640,000 to accommodate both junior and infant children. Previously pupils had to travel between two schools for meals and assembly. Headmistress at the time was Mrs Marion Randall.

In July 2002 a time capsule was unearthed at Polegate Primary School. It had been buried to mark the Queen's Silver Jubilee in 1977 and was opened during the Golden Jubilee celebrations. Items recovered included essays by pupils from that time and 1970s newspapers that were laid out for display.

More recently the swimming pool has been covered over and alterations carried out to the playground facilities.

BETWEEN THE WARS GROWTH

From the 1930s urban development around the A22 London to Eastbourne highway spread rapidly. Private estates were built north and south of the Lewes-Eastbourne railway line. After WWII local authority housing was constructed on the town's southern edge, with private housing limited to the construction of small bungaloid estates rounding off the built-up area. Construction of the first Polegate bypass commenced in the late 1930s and became the A22 main road.

Between the wars housing estates arrived at Southlands, Stud Farm and Brightling Road. After WWII many elderly residents bought these bungalows and several more estates were built between 1951 (3,564 residents) and 1971 notably with an influx of amenities. A new Post Office, telephone exchange, shops, library and school served the growing town. Many social groups started up, including the Community Association and Ratepayer's Association - typifying the on-going strengths of social life.

It was not until 1939 that growing Polegate became a civil parish comprising of 1,677 acres, taking land from neighbouring parishes of Hailsham, Jevington, Willingdon and Westham. Polegate officially came into being on April 1st 1939 with a new Town Council. Earlier adjustments to parish boundaries meant that some of this area was formerly from parts of Folkington and Wilmington.

More recently Polegate had acquired something of a granny image, being popular for retirement situations either in private residences or in nursing homes. Perhaps the younger generation got the message though and found the town's location at the foot of the South Downs and close to the sea and major retail outlets to their general liking. A town in transit perhaps? Now how many people can say that they have lived here all their life?

Whereas the railways originally dominated the community it is now the roads infrastructure that has dictated the growth of Polegate.

URBAN EXPANSION

The population by 1994 had grown to 7,890 and was still rising. About this time boundary changes threatened to divide the parish back amongst its neighbours, Hailsham and Eastbourne. To secure its continued existence Polegate became a town, with a Mayor and Town Council and chambers situated on the recreation ground alongside Wannock Road.

The now B2247 passing through Polegate splits housing areas in the north from the High Street facilities to the south. This former A27 thoroughfare carried large volumes of traffic during the summer months in particular, with visitors to resorts along the coast. This aspect added to local traffic, commuters and school runs, became a serious problem for the town and it was not until 2002 that the bypass was opened after two years construction work. Extension westerly of the A27 remains a contentious issue, the Beddingham flyover being the latest stop-gap measure.

Housing developers have plans with local authorities for urban expansion with a new township around the Cophall Farm acres. Under discussion are a new school and a second railway station as Polegate Parkway absorbing acres of Abbotts Wood, to meet government criteria for new homes. Other sites of contentious housing development are the Hindslands and Dittons Wood acres.

Local employment is often found in the neighbouring towns, public service industries, on factory estates, in hotels and farming and varied hospital units. Increasingly many people use Polegate for commuting to London and the suburbs for employment and some travellers acknowledge that Polegate railway facilities are more convenient than using Eastbourne station, whilst nearby Stone Cross warrants its own station again.

Polegate may have started out as a settlement around Polegate Junction railway network. The railways have declined in service and now bold new motorways border the town. Increasingly more people are beginning to appreciate Polegate's semi-rural location with its ease of access to the coast and neighbouring towns.

POLEGATE PARISH COUNCIL

The first election of Parish Councillors took place on December 4th 1895, with twenty-eight candidates for twelve vacancies at Hailsham and three for Polegate. It was not until 1939 that Polegate became a civil parish containing 1,687 acres, taking land from the ancient parishes of Hailsham, Westham. Willingdon and Jevington. Then during the 1980s the village became a town when there were moves to amalgamate local authorities in the name of economy. Hence a political move was undertaken.

One of the Residents Association councillors, of both the parish and Wealden District Council, investigated the dilemma and found that if they simply altered parish to town Polegate would keep and name and individuality. Alternatively south of the vital railway line would have become part of Willingdon Parish and the north district part of Westham Council.

The creation of Polegate Town Council was overwhelmingly approved by its members in July 1985. The previous month they voted to keep their 329 footpath lights on until 1.00am, because of concern for the safety of local residents

Fifteen councillors administer Polegate Town Council and they are elected for a four year term. In 1987 Polegate had no council offices and all the immediate records were kept by the Town Clerk, whilst the ESCC County Archivist kept all previous and older records.

The population by 1994 had grown to 7,890 residents and was increasing. It was at this time that proposed boundary changes threatened to divide the parish among its larger neighbours of Hailsham and Eastbourne. To secure its continued existence Polegate became a town a with Mayor, Town Council and Council Chambers situated on the recreation ground in Wannock Road.

After the May 1997 national elections residents awoke to find that Conservative MP Tim Rathbone was ousted, after twenty-three years, by Liberal Democrat newcomer Norman Baker who has continued to represent the community in a commendable role.

YOUTH CLUBS

Polegate Youth Club has a chequered past, having moved around the locale variously over the years. The Rev. Harry Parsons regrettably had to close the St John's Church Youth Club in the summer of 1957 because of bad behaviour. At this time Geoff Maynard opened his Tudor Cafe on the Lewes Road, these premises eventually became the Thoroughbred Inn. Whilst open for evening meals he installed a small nine record jukebox. Only a few people frequented the place for meals, whereas some twenty teenagers came to listen to the pop songs of the day.

Within this group he formed a members committee and the club became the Tudor Young People's Club, with over a hundred members. In the dozen years that the club flourished only three people were expelled for bad behaviour. Activities included darts, table tennis, bar billiards, pin-table and other such offerings. Film shows, talks, discussions and visits from the Vicar of Hampden Park the Rev. Donald Carpenter. At least three times each year a double-decker Southdown bus was hired for excursions to Southend, London or Lewes Bonfire Night etc. Also over four consecutive years they presented a pantomime in St John's Church hall.

When the Tudor Cafe was sold the youth club continued at the Community Centre under a Warden/Youth leader financed by ESCC. When this project came to an end the club ran for a further three years lead by volunteers, before activities terminated in the 1960s. More recently a youth club run by Geraldine Gurr met in the Reg Shingleton Amenity Centre in the Co-op car park. Unfortunately in 2000 this was forced to close as the building was decreed unsafe and was dismantled.

The youth organisation ran a mini bus that took youngsters on leisure trips and educational visits. Another building was promised, but as the council personnel changed so did their policies and no alternative building has been provided as a youth club. A church youth club used to meet in St John's Church on Friday evenings, this ran until 2000 when Stephen Pratt was youth leader. This group ran for a year, but in 2002 they closed and no other youth leader has come forward.

POLEGATE COMMUNITY CENTRE

The town is widely known for its convivial nature, even if the world stops us in the railtracks every time those crossing gates come down. Eight years of local planning, scheming, fund-raising frustration and sheer hard work by members of the Polegate Community Association bore fruition in 1969 when the gleaming new Polegate Community Centre was officially declared open by Mr T. Lydden Gardner - a Polegate resident for twenty-one years. Then in November 1975 a new social club extension was in full use as the Windsor Club premises, representatives of brewers Watney Mann pulling the first pint.

Today it is difficult to imagine a better used facility than the complex of rooms that are our central social outlet. Usage of the Windsor Club for recreation and a variety of local events, like elections, is backed up a scenario that currently encompasses:

Monday morning: Playgroup - all ages. Afternoon: Senior Citizens, Willingdon School of Dancing, Bowls. Evening: Bingo, Windsor Club Darts, Willingdon School of Dancing.

Tuesday morning: Playgroup, Polegate Sketching Group. Afternoon: Luncheon Club, Bowls. Evening Table Tennis, Drama Group.

Wednesday morning: Playgroup, Parents and Toddlers. Afternoon: Bowls, Over 50's Table Tennis. Evening: Table Tennis, Weightwatchers, Keep Fit, Electric Car Club.

Thursday morning: Playgroup. Afternoon: Luncheon Club, Bowls. Evening: Sequence Dancing Club, Drama Group.

Friday morning: Playgroup, Bowls, Yoga. Afternoon: Bowls, Whist Club, Willingdon School of Dancing. Evening: Beaver Scouts, Cub Scouts, Scouts.

Saturday morning: Coffee Morning, Karate.

Sunday afternoon: Windsor Windfall.

Monthly Meetings: Polegate Ladies' Circle, Polegate Wine & Social Club, the London Transport Retired Staff Association, Eastbourne Orchid Society, Southdown (Evening) Polegate WI.

POLEGATE TWINNING ASSOCIATION

Polegate has been twinned with Appen in Germany since 1981 and Saintry-Sur-Seine in France since 1991. The aims of town twinning are to promote and develop people in different countries and their ways of life. The Polegate Twining Association is an independent group run by a very active committee on which the Town Council has a representative. No funding is received from the council, but each time an exchange visit takes place the host country can apply for a grant from the European Union to assist with expenses.

The Twinning Association has about seventy members who take part in regular social events, such as a Burns Night celebrations, bingo, beetle drives, jumbles sales, coffee mornings and table sales to raise money to entertain overseas guests. Every two or three years Polegate receives a party from Appen for several days. Visitors stay in members homes and join in a varied programme of visits to places of interest and evening social activities.

In 1991 Polegate marked their tenth anniversary of twinning with Appen by inviting representatives of Appen and their East German twin town of Neukalen to meet the Mayor and Councillors from Saintry-Sur-Seine all here in Polegate.

Appen is situated about 10km south west of Appen in Kreis Pinneberg. Unlike Polegate it can trace its history back over 750 years. The area is noted for tree nurseries and for the cultivation of roses. It has a population of over 3,500 people living in the trio of villages Appen, Appen-Etz and Appen Unterglinde. Their council offices, school, shops and sports centre are all in Appen, while the church lies mid-way between the three residential areas. The church house and hall are both in Appen where one of the older farm houses has been converted into a community hall.

Saintry-Sur-Seine lies on the river Seine about 40km south east of Paris in the department of L'Essone. It is largely a dormitory area for Parisians and for Ivry that is an industrial town some 8km away. Saintry is interested in school exchange and not in social contact, which Polegate enjoys.

THE CUCKOO TRAIL

A fresh aspect of leisure came to Polegate in the 1980s with the creation of the Cuckoo Trail, although to some people recalling 1930s values of exploring the local countryside the resurgence of rambling and cycling activities may have seemed ironic.

The Polegate to Hailsham railway line opened in 1849 and extended to Heathfield in 1880. The service was well used as late as 1961, only to fall victim to Dr Beeching's programme of railway closures. Passenger services had ceased on the Eastbourne to Heathfield line by September 1968. During 1981 Wealden District Council and ESCC had formerly acquired redundant railway land south of Heathfield that was used as a public path.

The title Cuckoo Trail is derived from the Cuckoo Fair held at Heathfield on April 14th and October 16th annually. This in turn originates from folklore that on the first day of spring the old woman of Heffle released a Cuckoo from her basket at the April 14th fair. This legend also relates to hearing the bird very early each year along the railway line

The unmanaged railway terrain had deteriorated considerably and it was not until 1990 that Wealden announced a scheme with Sustrans (Sustainable transport) to rejuvenate the land as a green lane for walkers, cyclists and with some sections for horse riders. Sustrans is the national charity specialising in public tracks over dis-used railways and they entered into partnership with local authorities to start work in mid 1992 at Heathfield.

The more popular busy stretch between Hailsham and Polegate opened in autumn 1992 and in mid 1993 the Cuckoo Trail from Heathfield to Polegate was completed. On-going tangent activity off the trail has established links towards the coast with a network of other such leisure tracks. Notably the extension south towards Eastbourne and Hastings, plus the links westerly towards Lewes.

In May 1993 a dozen benches were placed along the Cuckoo Trail. The benches are made from local oaks blown down during the Great Storm of 1987.

POLEGATE WINDMILL

One of the more attractive impressions of Polegate is the windmill that was built in 1817 to replace an earlier wooden mill that blew down in a gale. The current tower mill was constructed in rendered brick. The mill, known as Park Croft Mill, continued to operate by wind power until 1941 when the fantail was damaged beyond repair. Electricity driven power took over to drive the crushing and grinding plant to meet the needs of animal feed flowing for local farmers.

In 1962 miller Ephraim Ovenden retired and he put the mill up for sale. In that year Eastbourne and District Preservation Society was formed and they campaigned for the mill to be preserved. An appeal was launched to raise £3,500 for its purchase and restoration and by 1965 the mill became the property of the society. Today the mill buildings are a hive of activity with many social involvements.

It was in May 2004 Wealden District Council received plans to improve the mills structure after a grant of £40,000 had been achieved from the Heritage Lottery Fund. A four stage rejuvenation headed Operation Weathershield will ensure the mills future. Sited in a now urban environment, on the boundary between Polegate and Lower Willingdon, the landmark mill is at times referred to as either Polegate windmill, or Willingdon windmill - originally Park Croft mill.

WANNOCK WATERMILL

The Seymour family owned both the watermill and the windmill. Henry Thomas, who lived between 1809-1885, once owned the mill and was the son of James and Ann Thomas of Sidely mill near Bexhill. Aged 17 years he became apprenticed to Joseph Seymour who owned Wannock watermill around 1826 and Henry went on to marry the miller's daughter named Phillis Seymour. The couple had three children: George was born in 1834, Thomas in 1835 and Mary Ann during 1839. Henry and Phillis lived at Wannock House, portraits of them can be seen at Polegate windmill. Their eldest son George moved to Strawberry Gardens and Streame Cottage at Wannock.

The lower mill was erected in 1883 and was demolished as recently as 1975. The wheel was 16ft diameter and six foot in width. The mill and overshot wheel and shaft drove three pairs of stones through an iron pit wheel, wallower and spur wheel, with a wooden upright shaft. The building was part brick and flint rubble, with brick quorns and dressings with half-nipped gabled roof. The mill remained working up to the 1950s.

The water wheel is now at Wateringbury in Kent. The mill pond was drained in 1959 and in-filled for housing development as Mill Race. The mill was demolished during the 1960s as part of the estate encompassing Croft Close, Farmlands Way, Mill Lane, Mill Race, Mill Stream Gardens, Old Mill Road, Park Croft and Watermill Close. Mill stream flows under Farmlands Avenue and Farmlands Way.

MORNINGS MILL

Mornings Mill Farm, like Polegate windmill, lies on the boundary between Polegate and Willingdon. As the demarcation area has changed over the years, so Mornings Mill is included in this account. The better known farm complex, off the main Eastbourne Road, was built during the 1800s and has been in the ownership of the Vine family for generations.

Prior to this period the farm was sited further away over the current railway track and comprised of a farm, a large watermill and support buildings. Some years ago an intriguing geophysical survey was conducted across this land and evidence of the farm complex and watermill emerged. The former pond of the watermill was so extensive that it extended over the now railway line route.

The ditch running alongside these fields is shown on Ordnance Survey maps as Mill Ditch. It is hard to ascertain where the farm and mill actually stood, as no evidence remains of the activities there. Apart from the middle of the field, where bull rushes flourish, an aura of the land contours suggest that some buildings once stood there - bordering Polegate.

More recently the lush Mornings Mill pastures have been in the news as the potential building site for hundreds of new homes, but that project has been put on hold.

POLEGATE LIBRARY

In 1929 the East Sussex County Council established a minor centre in Polegate. In 1951 Hailsham and Polegate libraries were transferred to East Sussex County Council control and the library at Polegate was housed in a classroom in the primary school at the old 1894 roadside school building. The library was staffed two volunteers and was open on Tuesday and Friday evenings and Saturday mornings. This service continued until the opening of the new Polegate Branch Library.

The new library opened on October 12th 1968. The facility is conveniently situated close to the Community Centre, Primary and Junior Schools and the High Street. The prefabricated single storey structure has an area of some 3,500 square feet and the car park was built to take thirty vehicles. An addition came with the mobile library van. The parking area now includes various recycling containers that residents ardently support.

In March 2001 the library re-opened after a major refit. It had been re-painted, carpeted and revised heating equipment installed. The premises had been closed for a month. Numerous on-going additions have been made to the library facilities over the years, the latest being availability of computer units to cater for the pace of new technology.

Perhaps ironically some people, making use of the library for computer activities, now find the time to extend their interests and whatever by making use of the books on the library shelves. Whereas in the past they may have dismissed use of the library facilities.

ESCC operate two mobile library units. The one operating from Polegate covers a wide area during the weekly runs. Starting from Wivelsfield Green the route covers Ditchling, Plumpton, Cooksbridge and Ringmer. Next day Alfriston to East Hoathly is visited and the week progresses to Framfield, Chelwood Gate, Udimore, Crowborough and Buxted.

Production of this archive would not have been possible, as and when it has, without access to certain files at Polegate Library to confirm dates, personalities, locations and activities.

SOME NOTABLE HOUSES AND COMMERCIAL PREMISES

As wealthy families sought desirable homes bordering Eastbourne and its developing resort facilities. Polegate became a popular venue to set up home. Some notable properties, now alas long gone, were Cranbrook Villa owned by Henry Leopold Mendell. Hollyhurst with Mrs Arrowsmith. Maryon Villa of Mrs Turner, Park Croft with Charles Baker, Peel House of Edward Davy, Sunny Dene of Henry Marks.

SOUTHDOWN HALL

Caleb Diplock, born in Rotherfield in 1818, became a resourceful and prosperous business man. He founded the Lion Brewery in Eastbourne, the site more recently having been occupied as the Southdown bus depot in Pevensey Road. Lion Brewery was for many years controlled by Diplock, Son & Pepler. (Pepler became associated with Eric Gill at Ditchling and innovative design and printing techniques.) The Lion concern at one time owned some seventeen public houses in the district. Dominating the brewery roof was the large statue of a lion. The brewery was demolished in 1920 and the lion made its way to the grounds of Folkington Manor.

Southdown Hall was built as an imposing family home for Caleb Diplock in 1873. Sadly with the passage of time, and fortune, Southdown Hall and its ten acres of gardens came under the auctioneers hammer on August 10th 1936. A sale notice announcing the dispersal indicated that Southdown Hall was a commodious country residence with extensive grounds and was suitable for development as a private hotel or school. Also in the sale was Wannock Coppice Farm with house and out-buildings, land ripe for building. Together with a market garden holding in Langney. The whole being about 104 acres.

A legacy of that period are a pair of former lodge houses that fronted Southdown Hall. West Lodge is extant tucked away alongside the junction of the busy A2022 and the A27 highways. A similar property named East Lodge is extant opposite AutoWise at the end of Old Mill Drive.

OSBORNE HOUSE

William Henry Attwood built elegant Osborne House in 1869-1870 in the style of Queen Victoria's regal Osborne House in the Isle of Wight. His ground floor rooms were richly decorated in gold leaf and he had a private chapel on the western side of the property (now the site of a bungalow). A ship's bell relic stood outside and fragments of statuettes from the chapel have been found in the grounds.

In 1925 Osborne House appeared as Lot 25 in an auction, with vacant possession of over an acre. The 1925 auction included the neighbouring house as Lot 21. This property was known as Albert Cottage, in the tenancy of George Levett. By 1962 the property had had its time and was costly to maintain and it was demolished. A block of terraced flats named Osborne Court, in Albert Road, were built on the site of Attwood's once grand Italianate villa.

An adjacent coach house had been added and was used as such until the main house went. The building was subsequently converted into a private dwelling by a Mr Lloyd who used the coach house as a museum for his butterfly collection. The ship's bell made its way to the coach house that with the former stables are extant facing the main road and Albert Road respectively.

BERNHARD BARON COTTAGE HOMES

The neat retirement estate of dwellings named Bernhard Baron Cottage Homes were built in 1937, under a Trust contained in the will of Caleb Diplock who passed away March 23rd 1936. However his documents were the subject of some dispute, finally on June 21st 1944 it was determined by the House of Lords (affirming the decision of the Court of Appeal) that this Trust was void for the uncertainty of its wording. The original cottages on the site were known as Diplock's Cottages and sited opposite the entrance to Southdown Hall. The distinctive statute of a stag came from Southdown Hall.

In September 1945 the property was purchased by the Religious Society of Friends (the Quakers) with the aid of contributions that included a substantial grant from the Bernhard Baron Trust, in recognition of which the homes were named after the major benefactor. In March 1946 there were forty residents and five staff, but by May that year the wardens had a waiting list. In January 1948 Charles and Harriet Haworth became the third couple to serve as wardens at the homes and they remained there until April 1959. Next appointees were Geoffrey and Marcella Bowes who kept their positions until retirement in 1965. They were followed by Donald and Ida Tear between October 1965 and 1971.

The dozen flint cottages are laid out as self-contained units, the residents of which are expected to join others at least once a day in the main building. In September 1971 came two additions on loan. A pair of pet donkeys named Joy and Beauty occupied a field later named Donkey Field, but this has now been built over. A Wardens Cottage was added in 1968, along with subsequent on-going alterations and development at the estate.

The extensive grounds surrounding the homes once included tennis courts, but land was sold in late March 1973 as the Trustees of the Bernhard Baron Cottage Homes sought funding to create new cottages. Parcels of land were sold to Quality Homes Ltd and roads and homes were built as Barons Way, Bernhard Gardens and Hilary Close. Bernhard Baron had amassed a fortune as a cigarette manufacturer, but passed his goodwill onto local charitable causes.

THE DINKUM

The town's popular meeting place was originally named the Railway Arms circa 1847, but became the New Inn by 1900. There is reason to suggest that The Cottage next door had previously been a beer house.

The premises formerly underwent a name change in mid 1979. During WWI gas warfare colonial troops convalescing nearby at Chalk Farm would walk past, or frequent, the Polegate Inn and comment that it was fair dinkum. Locals adopted this reference and during the 1979 refurbishment Harvey's Brewery sportingly changed the name to The Dinkum. There cannot be any other hostelries with such an original name!

THE LONDON BRIGHTON & SOUTH COAST RAILWAY

The original Polegate station opened in June 1846, when the line from Lewes to Bulverhythe was completed, was sited 400 yards east of the present station. On June 27th that year the London Brighton & South Coast Railway Company completed the Hastings to London route via Brighton, by opening the line from Lewes to St Leonard's-on-Sea.

Polegate was only a hamlet at the time, but a station was erected at the inter-section of the railway track with the Eastbourne to Hailsham turnpike, mainly to serve passengers from these towns. Initially there was a weekly service of four trains each way. As the track ran inland direct, from Lewes towards Hastings, passengers for Eastbourne had to alight at Polegate and could board coaches like Daniel Burford's horse bus which met every train.

Branch lines to Hailsham and Eastbourne opened in May 1849 and Polegate became a junction. The loop to Eastbourne was over four miles long bearing right from Polegate with a falling gradient towards Hampden Park, where a station was built in 1888, then known as Willingdon Station. A spur line was subsequently added between Stone Cross and Hampden Park (Willingdon Junction), thus opening the way to Eastbourne.

The redundant northern aspect of the Polegate-Eastbourne-Hastings railway triangle was finally closed on January 6th 1969. Occasional trains ran across this top line until 1974 as an engineers siding to Stone Cross. More recently homes have been erected along the former railway track. Stone Cross Halt, that closed in 1905, was sited near the bridge over the B2104 from Lion Hill towards Friday Street. A new station serves traffic as Pevensey and Westham Station.

Passenger facilities at this first Polegate station were spartan, the waiting room measured 12ft x 8ft. Signalling by way of the Saxby and Farmer Absolute Block working was introduced in 1874. Polegate-Redgate Mill Junction (Eridge) was equipped with Hudson's Union of Harpers Block and Sykes Lock from 1880.

In 1851 the London Brighton & South Coast Railway joined up with a line laid by the South Eastern Railway from Ashford to St Leonards. The LBSCR trains had running powers over the Southern Eastern Railway to Hastings. By 1860 the service to Eastbourne had increased and the Hailsham route was now used separately. In the meantime the Willingdon loop had been opened in August 1871, allowing trains to run direct between Eastbourne and Hastings.

On April 5th 1880 the Hailsham line was extended in stages north to Heathfield and continuation to Eridge, Tunbridge Wells and in September gave Eastbourne a secondary route to London. This line became known as the Cuckoo Line by reason of Heathfield Cuckoo Fair held annually on April 14th. The original plan provided for trains from the Cuckoo Line to Eastbourne to run direct passing under the Polegate-Hastings Line. However in the event this was changed and a new Polegate station was built 400yds east of the original station so that trains from Hailsham could enter from the west and proceed to Eastbourne. Eastbourne junction was re-aligned.

This second Polegate station (now Buddies restaurant) opened on October 3rd 1881 with waiting rooms, refreshment facilities and other creature comforts. Notably track re-laying allowed direct running of Hailsham to Eastbourne trains in connection with the Cuckoo Line northern extension to Tunbridge Wells. Hampden Park station opened in 1888.

LOCAL PASSENGER SERVICES

At the period of LBSCR and early Southern Railway main line services from London ran either to Hastings detaching a portion at Polegate for Eastbourne, or to Eastbourne with a portion for Hastings. In the later years of steam traction both companies employed slip coaches. This system caused a few problems. Hastings & St Leonard's Weekly Mail and Times in January 1909 reported that an accident occurred on the 4.05 train from London to Eastbourne and Hastings near Polegate. The rear carriages of this train slipped for Hastings, whilst the front portion proceeded towards Eastbourne after slipping had taken place. The Eastbourne section was brought to a standstill owing to a defect in the air brake and the slipping carriages dashed into the standing train. There was some damage to the trains and the line was blocked, several persons were severely shaken.

The system was for each portion of the train to have a guard. On approaching Polegate the express train driver would slow slightly, the guard of the rear portion would operate a lever which released the coupling between the two portions. The driver would then accelerate away while the rear guard would gradually apply his brakes and bring the rear section to a standstill at the platform.

Obviously this could not apply in the up direction towards London. Other services were mainly stopping trains between Brighton and Hastings, one or two of which ran on to or from Ashford. On the Cuckoo Line trains ran either to Hailsham, Heathfield or Tunbridge Wells, one or two conveyed carriages for London via Oxted detached at Eridge and were taken forward by a train from Brighton or Uckfield.

One interesting train in the 1920s/1930s era was the Sunday Pullman service which left Victoria at 10.45am arriving at Eastbourne at 12.10pm in time for a long lunch at a smart hotel, followed by an afternoon stroll on the promenade - with tea on the return Pullman leaving at 5.20pm. In 1935 the main lines were electrified, but this had little effect on the appearance of Polegate station.

In 1975 the platform canopies were removed, along with many platform buildings. Some extra passenger shelters were installed and electricity replaced the gas lighting system. This Georgian second station, built in 1881, was to survive in service until 1986.

GOODS TRAINS

During the time of LBSCR and early Southern Railway services Polegate was a fairly important freight centre and boasted a small marshalling yard. Goods from the Midlands and North arrived via Battersea, other London traffic came from the Willow Walk (Bricklayers Arms) site. There were goods depots both on express goods trains to Eastbourne and Hastings. At Polegate wagons would drop off for stations along the Cuckoo Line - for Pevensey, Bexhill and Hampden Park - with many wagons going in reverse direction.

Traffic from the Western counties and South Wales came either via Northwood Yard (Croydon) or along the coast from Chichester and Brighton. Southern Railway ran a nightly express goods train from Eastleigh to Ashford, calling at principal stations like Polegate. With the postwar decline of freight traffic Polegate's marshalling yard closed in the early 1950s, the work being deployed between Eastbourne and Lewes. There were also trains carrying such goods as newspapers, parcels and cattle.

TRAMWAY ADJOINING THE BRANCH LINE

A curios earthworks industrial legacy may be found alongside the Cuckoo Trail, south of the Old Loom Mill facility at OS 586068. A siding created half way between Polegate and Hailsham was opened under an agreement of 1899 between LBSCR and Eastbourne House & Trading Company. Known as Greatfield Siding the works is referred to in the 1912 Railway Clearing House of Stations.

This tramway, or narrow gauge railway, ran west across fields to a brickworks created between Nightingale Farm and Summer Hill. In 1921 the Polegate Brick & Tile Co were authorised to take-over the siding under the same 1899 agreement. A LBSCR freight locomotive, that had previously shunted to Hailsham, moved the materials. The key for unlocking the siding points being obtained from Hailsham signal box, but returned to the Polegate box.

By the time the 1938 RCH stations handbook was published the site had been acquired by the Maidenhead Brick & Tile Co, but by 1950 rail traffic had ceased. The siding was derelict and tracks were disconnected from the main line, although the lever frame artefact that operated the siding remained in situ for some time. Works at the depot finally terminated in 1970, although a track is marked on current Ordnance Survey Explorer maps. The site had been run by Southdown Tileries Ltd from 1925-1934, when it passed to the Keymer Brick & Tile Company that was then in time

POLEGATE & DISTRICT RAILWAY TIME CHART

June 27th 1846. London and Brighton Railway opened their line from Lewes to St Leonard's (Bulverhythe).

June 27th 1846. Polegate's first railway station opened to the public.

July 27th 1846. London & Brighton Railway Co amalgamated with the London & Croydon Co to form the London, Brighton & South Coast Railway.

October 1st 1847. Keymer Junction-Lewes opened. London passengers no longer have to go to Brighton.

May 14th 1849. Polegate-Eastbourne and Polegate-Hailsham lines opened. Polegate becomes a junction. A second signal box sited nearby to operate the junction.

August 1st 1871. The Willingdon-Stone Cross spur opened. Through trains now able to call at Eastbourne.

April 5th 1880. The Hailsham-Heathfield, Cuckoo Line, opened.

September 1st 1880. Heathfield-Redgate (Eridge) line opens, creating alternative Eastbourne-London link.

October 3rd 1881. Polegate's second station opened. The Eastbourne and Hailsham lines were re-aligned.

1899. A siding on the Polegate-Hailsham line was created under an agreement between LBSCR and Eastbourne House Land & Trading Co. Named Greatfield Siding it is referred to in the 1912 Railway Clearing House of Stations files. Some time later the firm ceased trading and the siding became derelict.

January 1st 1923. The grouping of railway companies. LBSCR becomes part of Southern Railway. **July 7th 1935.** Electrification of the main line.

January 1st 1948. Nationalisation. Southern Railway absorbed as part of British Railways.

February/March 1963. Polegate crossing gates replaced by barriers. Up and over instead of push gates.

June 14th 1965. Redgate Mill (Eridge)-Hailsham line closed to passenger traffic.

September 9th 1968. Hailsham-Polegate line closed. Earlier line to Stone Cross also closed.

January 6th 1969. Direct route to Hastings officially closed and up line rails lifted shortly afterwards.

March 1970. Demolition of the first Polegate station. Including signal box, turntable, goods shed, granary, engine shed and the Junction Hotel.

October 1971. Up-sidings lifted.

1974. Down Hastings direct line lifted at Polegate end. Polegate ceases to be a junction.

November/December 1975. Demolition of canopy and most platform buildings at second station (Buddies). Gas lighting replaced by electricity.

May 25th 1986. Polegate's third station officially opened by Ian Gow MP.

absorbed by Maidenhead Brick & Tile Co in the late 1920s, but continued to operate under its own name. Excavations there made a series of lakes named Amazon Wood that are now popular with local fishermen.

In March 1993 some 200 people attended a meeting, backed by councillors, and fought off plans to re-activate the tile works and clay extraction operations at Nightingale Farm. Currently the site is signed Tarmac Southern Ltd, Eastbourne Mortar & Concrete Plant. *Maureen Copping.*

POLLY ARCH BRIDGE

Another local remnant of railway evolution can be found as Polly Arch, off the on-going residential development from Lynholm Road. The bridge, that bears no foundation stone or dating, was built about 1846 when LBSCR laid tracks direct between Lewes and Hastings. The bridge became known colloquially as Polly Arch (shortened from Polegate) and the name has stuck. Curiously the 57ft long structure came up for auction a few years ago and was sold to an anonymous German buyer for £5,000. In October 1998 it was again auctioned. Bidding began at £2,000 and rose steadily, being hammered at £4,000, again the owner sought to remain anonymous. The tenure being vacant possession and advertised as . . . be the envy of your friends!

LOCAL BRICKFIELDS

Between 1890-1933 some five brickfields were established locally, notably at the western end of Brook Street, now Brookside Avenue. Stephen Message acquired this land in 1880 to use as a brickyard. Houses were constructed nearby, but he was unable to sustain this enterprise by 1899. So many properties remained unsold, there were unpaid bills and he was enforced to sell the brickyard. William Beeny, a local coal merchant, also opened a brickyard alongside the railway.

Invariably a property developer would acquire land to be used as a brickfield, close to the site where he proposed to develop properties. Many brickyards used the railway network to ferry bricks. Some firms installed narrow gauge railway lines to link up with the main lines to transport their stocks. Various brickyards are to be seen on the maps included in this account.

TRANSPORT AND ROAD WORKS

There is reference to a horse bus running from the Polegate station in 1845/1846 operated by Daniel Burford. This service functioned between Polegate and Eastbourne until August 2nd 1871 and a number of other operators were offering similar routes.

After WWI the main form of transport was horse drawn and carriers offered flys, horse-drawn carts and carriages, that ferried people and goods around the community. The main bus company in Polegate was started by Henry Twine in 1924 and he continued for many years until his business was acquired by the Southdown Bus Company. Twine shrewdly moved on to property development and is said to have built around 600 homes and commercial premises locally. He had purchased his first bus for £7.10s. (£7.50), the vehicle seated fourteen people and provided a regular service between Jevington and Eastbourne by way of Polegate crossroads and Willingdon village.

To ply for hire within the County Borough of Eastbourne a licence from Eastbourne Watch Committee had to be obtained for the vehicle. The first buses were fitted with solid tyres, which provoked harsh riding conditions, that were particularly so passing between Wannock and Jevington. The then road repairer lived at Jevington and was kept rather occupied repairing the chalky downland un-surfaced highway, enabling Henry's solid tyred charabanc to maintain a regular schedule.

As trade grew so did Henry Twine's fleet. Their second omnibus was also second hand, but had pneumatic tyres at the front to smooth out the rural journeys. The third bus had pneumatic tyres all round and their fourth addition, a Dodge, was actually purchased new. Finally their was a thirty-two seater Dennis in Twine's fleet. Petrol came from Ernest Waghorn's garage, where AutoWise now stands. Waghorn had grown up with the motor trade and could turn his hand to any maintenance or repairs. He undertook all the tasks involved keeping Twine's fleet mobile, working any hours to keep the service running.

One popular bus route was from Polegate crossroads by way of

Wannock to Jevington, back to Polegate and then on through Willingdon village, before the days of the 1930s A22 thoroughfare. At Jevington the journey finished outside the cottages now trading as the Hungry Monk, where a Mrs Finch ran tea rooms. When Jevington School started it took children from Wannock, but it 1927 that school closed and Henry's bus was contracted to take the youngsters to Willingdon school.

Henry meanwhile acquired property named Staleen in Dittons Road to house his fleet. This site later became Robin Bank and the Waterhouse Coach depot. As competition escalated Southdown buses were pitched to run just before Twine's service. With other local operators Twine protested their situation, but Southdown Co bought out their opposition and for many decades held a monopoly - until the 1980s when small bus firms again took to the county highways in a competitive mode.

BYPASS HIGHWAYS

The first bypass road was built in the 1930s to carry A22 traffic southwards from Polegate crossroads into Eastbourne, this road has now been re-classified the A2022. The first time a revised A27 route running through northern aspects of Polegate arose in the 1975 East Sussex Structure Plan and in 1979 a feasibility study was carried out into vital potential routes between Dittons and Eastbourne town centre.

East Sussex County Council considered a route between the existing A27 at Dittons Wood and Willingdon Drive. Also in 1979 the Department of Transport was looking at bypass routes around Polegate and Pevensey. Amid a drastic governmental policy of road building cutbacks it was with considerable surprise locally that plans for the Polegate bypass were announced.

Highway management was considered as being undertaken by private enterprise, with the government paying back the developers over ensuing years allied to the volume of use. The second bypass came about after it had been at the planning stages for over a decade before works even commenced, completion coming in 2002 well ahead of the targeted time.

In the very early stages ESCC took into account environmental issues and the existing ecology was surveyed in July 1990. All the fields beside the route had been arable pastures or for haymaking and some were re-seeded and young trees planted out. Some wildlife were re-located - rare Great Crested Newts were moved outside the construction area, bats were found new nesting and roosting boxes and small mammals protected from the bypass by wire mesh installed beside the road.

Mixed hedgerows bordering the fields were mature and dense with a variety of species providing natural habitats. Such areas featured woodlands with mature oak, ash, beech, sycamore, maple, horse chestnut, lime and occasional conifer trees. Consideration of replacing woodland around banking had to be accommodated in the bypass - such are the demands of modern road-making. A hyped dual carriageway, a road to nowhere, had been completed some years previously, linking Dittons with Lottbridge Drove which subsequently all tied in extremely well with the incessant traffic flow.

The dual lane 7.30m wide bypass joins the 1930s bypass on the A22 at Cophall Farm, running east to the recently finished Pevensey bypass at Dittons. A replacement Cophall Farm house had been built some years earlier further west and the older farmhouse remained boarded up. Planning applications had been lodged for some years prior to the roundabout being built for a service station and motel type facilities off the roundabout.

In June 2002 the long-awaited bypass was opened. People in Polegate could breath a huge sigh of relief as the loading on local roads was drastically reduced. Residents of Hailsham Road and Station Road must feel an uncanny spell has descended upon them after years of heavy traffic bounding past their doors.

Transport consultants Halcrow had proposed building another road through Honey Farm to connect Cophall roundabout with the A27. This would have created a large triangle of open land with main roads along two sides and the railway along the other - the Polegate triangle - but this would have created an even larger scale roadworks scheme.

DIPLOCK'S WOOD - HIGH COURT CASE

Just over a quarter of a mile south of Polegate crossroads, on the road to Wannock on the western side, there is a small wood known variously as Diplock's Wood or Wannock Coppice. In recent years this woodland became neglected and a dumping place for the neighbourhood. Polegate Parish Council has considered the problems of the wood for some years. They included the view that if they were to take a lease on the area it could be tidied up and kept neat and would become a pleasant place of resort for the public.

The grounds were part of the Diplock estate and came into dispute upon his demise. Caleb Diplock junior made a will in 1919 which, proved in the year of his death, showed his gross estate to be £527,936 on which death duties of £178,587 were paid. Over £300,000 remained. After specific bequests had been met the residue of about a quarter of a million pounds was to be given to such charities as his executors selected. This was done and the whole estate distributed. Wannock Coppice was offered to Hailsham Rural District Council early in 1937 . . . to perpetuate the name of Caleb Diplock in the neighbourhood - with the proviso that there should be public access . . . that the Council shall employ a custodian to prevent nuisance and preserve the wood and that the name be changed from Wannock Coppice to Diplock Wood. On July 31st 1937 the wood was to be open to the public for the first time having been cleared and paths, railings and gates constructed.

The iron railings, that some people may remember, along the roadside were first erected in 1924 as part of the bargain Caleb struck with the Eastbourne District Council when they took the edge of the wood to widen the road to eighteen feet. These iron railings, similar to those along Black Path, were taken as scrap during WWII. Then a shock was received.

In January 1940 his relatives began an action to have the will declared void for uncertainty and to have the estate distributed as if the testator had died intestate. The following year the Master of the Rolls made an order . . . that the residue had not been disposed of because of the vagueness of the phrase charitable or benevolent. That the testator had not meant to bring non-charitable objects within the ambit of the powers of the executors. An appeal to the House of Lords in 1944 failed, but the defendants (the executors and beneficiaries) did not give up and brought the matter to the court again in 1947, but it still failed.

Hailsham District Council together with all the other residue beneficiaries, was required to pay the cash value of their inheritance into court. Accordingly £800 was paid in 1947 for the wood. After this there was an attempt to call the wood the Rowland Gwynne Wood, but this never became common usage. Rowland Gwynne of Folkington Manor and Wootton became Chairman of the Hailsham District Council throughout the whole of the period (in fact from 1924 to 1947).

The government, in the guise of the National Health Service, still continued to fight until 1950 when their test case against returning £4,000 given to Westminster Hospital failed. This test signalled the return of all the money given to hospitals - Guy's had received the largest sum, £20,000. Forty-eight people benefited eventually as the next-of-kin of the intestate.

In March 1977 the local council heard that a private firm had offered £700 for trees to be felled in the wood. Felling and clearance work had already commenced with volunteers involved. The parish council had taken over responsibility for the wood from Wealden Council the previous year.

By October 1985 Polegate Town Council had had enough of caring for Diplock's Wood. Council members decided to give Wealden District Council six months notice to end the licence they adopted in October 1976. Since these problems the coppice has become an established local facility, to be enjoyed by the public at large.

Vera Hodsoll.

GILBERT LEVETT AND DITTONS WOOD

By 1935 Gilbert Levett, having previously built several houses locally, decided to expand his activities and purchased land from the Duke of Devonshire through Compton Estates, the Duke's local Estate Office. He called his first house Fellands and this became his family home for the next sixty years, his daughter was born there in 1937. He went on to build three more houses on adjacent land and this sale made him financially secure.

He purchased further land from the Duke's estate fronting Pevensey Road, constructing some twenty houses and bungalows. He would have continued building there, but for the fortuitous bargain-price purchase of a run-down nursery adjacent to Fellands - large enough for a dozen bungalows. This new estate he named Nursery Close and his mother-in-law Mrs Andrews, bought the first bungalow. She lived there until a 1941 air raid that severely damaged the property, moving back to Fellands (where Levett had already built his own air raid shelter beside the house) after the repairs were completed, until she passed away in 1950.

The last of the Nursery Close homes were completed just after the outbreak of WWII in 1939. During the war years Gilbert Levett served in the local Royal Horse Artillery Territorial Army, becoming a Sergeant and Instructor of Motor Vehicles. He had volunteered to serve in the Regular Army, but the Medical Board refused to accept him, apparently due to a heart tumour. His next business activities continued with war work, constructing ARP shelters and supplying wood for domestic fuel.

In 1948 Gilbert Levett managed to secure Dittons Wood from the Duke of Devonshire's estates. The area had been a popular beauty spot, but Gilbert Levett planned to build a large, select, estate there when the woodland was cleared. Three hundred or so large and prime oak trees in the wood were cut down and sold. The resulting cordwood being converted into firewood logs.

The large tree stumps and roots left after the trees were felled had to be removed, but were proving an expensive operation and experts were called in. Duly armed with the proper authorisation Levett Builders regularly collected gelignite and detonators from a depot in Erith. The explosives were stored in a shed at Dittons Wood. On opening the store one morning a hole in the timber roof revealed overnight visitors had taken a considerable quantity of gelignite and detonators. The police duly arrived, thinking a terrorist group might have been involved - but that proved to be a false lead. After several weeks of diligent police work the guilty culprits, merely schoolboys, were found. A search of their homes uncovered enough gelignite to have blown a house apart. Their eventual court case produced a laughable sentence.

To loosen the roots holes were drilled into the tree stumps, explosives were inserted and electrically fired from a safe distance. Their Caterpillar tractors then speedily removed the roots. Even so, it took two months to clear the land. Then on the final day of blasting, with some surplus gelignite remaining, the usual number of cartridges was considerably increased in several of the roots - just for luck. The resulting heavy explosions produced spectacular showers of dirt and roots, which settled to reveal smoking holes - some of at least five feet deep, with not a root in sight.

The elation was short-lived, Gilbert Levett heard the explosion and fearing the worst the police quickly arrived. Local Police Sergeant Charlie Hopkins had been alerted by a telephone call. Fortunately the Sergeant was a family friend and had a good laugh, although Gilbert huffed and puffed a bit. The adjacent nursery's owner arrived on the scene carrying an enormous chunk of tree root, swearing and bitterly complaining. This great root and bits like it had smashed into a greenhouse, his staff would not work under the glass until the blasting stopped. He threatened legal action and it started to look ugly. However the Police Sergeant managed to calm the situation and some deft wallet-work by Gilbert Levett ended everything amicably.

Upon their return from a holiday Gilbert Levett concentrated on development of his Fellands home. During their world tour he had been taken ill, but no definite cause could be found. In the 1970s he had extensive medical tests which pointed to serious heart damage. Surgeons at Guy's Hospital fitted a replacement heart valve which was still working when he passed away in 1991.

In the late 1980s Gilbert Levett had received several serious offers, including one of £100,000, from large firms anxious to purchase Dittons Wood for their land banks. These were all rejected on advice from his accountants and solicitors.

During the early 1990s McAlpine Co wanted to buy Dittons Wood and adjacent land. The group offered a very attractive financial package to Gilbert Levett's widow and the other landowners concerned. After considerable investigations, by his widow's solicitors, they accepted the quite complex agreement and adjacent landowners followed suit, although the options had not been taken-up by McAlpine by 2001.

Extracted from Notes of the Life of Gilbert Levett, by Maurice F. Levett, Watford, May 2001.

OTHAM COURT

Polegate's oldest ancestral site, nestling on the parish borders, has an uncertain future. Several years ago the Otham Court property was acquired by the Ministry of Transport, prior to creation of the A27 bypass and it is currently occupied by a caretaker as strictly private property. At the time of writing, in autumn 2004, the property was under offer, after being advertised with a price guide of £1m by Smiths Gore of Petworth. The six bedrooms Grade II listed property is set in 12.86 acres.

It was in the year 1208 that a migration of monks took place, although the origins of Otham as an abbey lasted only twenty-eight years. Jordan, its first and only abbot, became the first of a long line of abbots of Bayham.

As an abbey-grange Otham Abbey, of the Premonstratensian canons, fulfilled a useful life through several centuries. Two or three canons were left behind, or sent back in relays, to superintend the work of the farm. Thus the chapel bell rang at daybreak for morrow-mass and at evening time for compline. Day by day men went forth to work and labour. Gradually the sour land became clean and into rich vegetable tilth.

Otham Abbey seen in the 1930s.

The monks of the Middle Ages were progressive and resourceful agriculturalists and the acres around Otham Court became amongst the richest and most fertile of the county.

A significant event was the re-building of the chapel about 1360. It stands now a poor little ruin, but observers may note deep silled windows, lovely head tracery, canopied sedillae, a piscina rated one of the best in Sussex. The garth on the south side where the cloister was and brick built-up door where the canons entered. On the west facing door the laity went in for prayers.

In 1526 the lights went out and the gold image with its silver accessories - once the pride and joy of folks around - was sent to swell the king's coffers at Westminster. The lands were first given to Cardinal Wolsey for his new college at Oxford, but soon the King took them back and they were sold and re-sold.

In the mid 1930s the owner was Colonel Rowland Gwynne of Folkington Manor and the chapel of St Laurence, though forlorn and desolate, did receive by his solitude timely repairs.

RESIDENTS RECOLLECTIONS

LETTER FROM CANADA

Two summers ago I attended a cricket match right here in Richmond, British Columbia, held between Polegate and Queensland. The Polegate ladies were a most welcoming committee and greeted myself with friendship. Returning to Polegate the seven children who arrived there with my parents were Talbot, myself Patricia, Ronald, Betty, Edward, Arthur and Dorothy. My four brothers all served during WWII and father during WWI. Talbot was in the RAF and became a Prisoner of War to the Japanese. Ronald was also in the RAF. Ted (Edward) in the RCAF and Arthur enlisted in the Royal Canadian Navy.

I wonder if there are any persons in Polegate who would now remember this large family who lived across the road from the school? It was there that I had my first canning, across the hand. I cannot recall what it was for, although it was probably quite all undeserved. When I visited the area on a recent trip to England it seemed to be all very built up and the station was quite different. I was the only one of the seven children born to our parents who remained single. I am eighty-four years of age now and hampered with arthritis in my fingers and feet. In later years genealogy has become a hobby and I found that I had a cousin living in Polegate, but she has passed away. I am also related to a couple in Wannock Drive. Our stay in Polegate was so short, but memorable.

Miss Patricia Knight, Richmond, British Columbia, Canada.
January 2004.

MY EARLY LIFE IN POLEGATE

Some of my childhood was dominated by the war years and I remember spending night after night in the shelter listening to the roar of planes above. I recall seeing bombs falling out of the planes on a beautiful cloudless day and they fell on the Southlands Estate causing death and destruction.

My father did WD (war damage) work and he would come home exhausted after spending many hours digging in bombed buildings for people - he was also in Polegate Home Guard unit and his comments when he was getting ready for duty are unrepeatable - something to do with couldn't guard a pussy. During the build up to D-Day many Americans and Canadian convoys passed through Polegate and the soldiers would throw out sweets to the children standing on the side of the roads - I was there as often as possible. On VE day we were given a holiday from school which pleased us greatly.

There were very few vehicles on the roads after the war and often when we came out from the 'big school on the bridge' we would all join hands, run, skip, or roller skate down the middle of Station Road to the railway station. There was nothing for the children to do in Polegate and we spent most of our time playing in our gardens or on the paths and roadways. I was a member of Polegate Tennis Club which had two grass courts opposite the entrance to the Recreation Ground. I would spend every summer evening playing there and in 1950, 1953 and 1954 I won the Ladies Singles Cup which was presented by Mrs Miller who lived at Folkington Manor.

When Harry Parsons became Vicar of Polegate he started a Youth Club and a Junior Church which was very well received by the young people as it meant we had somewhere to go in the evening. He also branched out with the annual Sunday School treat and instead of it being held in a field at Polegate he laid on a day trip to Chessington Zoo or Littlehampton. Often there were five or six coaches filled with happy parents and children who really had a wonderful day out.

Many of the parents were shocked when the vicar appeared on the sands at Littlehampton in a bathing costume and were even more shocked when we members of the Junior Church buried him in the sand until his head was showing. Happy days!

I had a bicycle and I would go off on my own all day for rides around the area and my parents never worried as they knew I would turn up at tea time. In the hot weather we often used to paddle in the stream running near Polly Arch, although we were forbidden to do this which made it that much better. I have fallen in the stream many times and have taken most of my clothing off and hung it on a bush to dry, so that my mother didn't get to know where I had been.

Jeanne Fry, nee Levett, Polegate.

TALES FROM BLACK PATH

Our first railway station had been built in 1846, along with those at Glynde, Berwick, Pevensey and Bexhill, with only one platform when they first opened. Second platforms were provided slightly later to improve conditions. By the time the second station at Polegate was created in 1881 Eastbourne Chronicle was saying much the same as about the 1846 station . . . at the old station is one dismal waiting room, or an apology for such and it is far from being weatherproof. The new station was . . . more exposed to weather than was an old cattle-truck junction-like delapitated affair which has hitherto done duty as a railway station.

On the 1881 opening day it was reported that men . . . were still working on finishing touches to the station. Whilst others were completing the road by which the new station was to be approached by the up side, i.e. the popular black path created from railway engine ashes. Whether Black Path rejoiced in the appelation right from that time we shall never know, certainly it has been known as such for several generations. Although properly consolidated and levelled its surface was for many years merely crushed clinker turned out from the endless stream of steam locomotives.

The road was given a more permanent surface before WWII, but the footpath alongside the railings was still ashes into the 1950s. As a child I was forbidden to walk in the road after our next door neighbour had been knocked down and killed by a car whilst walking in the road. A dapper man given to flannels, and those pre-war part brown, part white brogues, he was not going to soil his footwear walking on the ashes. As for myself in sandals a shoe full of grit had to be shaken out at the path's end. Anyway by walking on the path one could drag a stick along the railings! How endless Black Path seemed. The only way to make it seem shorter was to keep an eye on the tops of the buildings along the north side of the line which appeared above the bank on which the line runs. First the end of the platform buildings and canopy, then the end of the platform, the water tank, the large signal box and then the granary and lastly the goods yard buildings with railway workers cottage. In Black Path itself there was only the old Junction Hotel building, which had long been given over to staff railway housing.

Usages at the first pair of stations are mere visions and the Black Path of memory is no more. The world of nature has retreated from Black Path beyond all recall.

Vera Hodsoll, former Branch Librarian, Polegate Library.

ARTISAN BROOK STREET

I moved into Polegate in 1963, my present wife in about 1960. She lived in Gilda Crescent, I bought a cottage in Brook Street - price £1,750. She rented a flat for 30/- a week. The cottages in Brook Street were built in two stages, the six in the middle were built in 1857 by a reverend somebody and sold to the railway for their staff. The rest were built in 1870 I think. The old original cottages had water wells halfway down the gardens, one well per two cottages. The well between Nos 36-38 was still there in 1970, but capped. Most of the people in the street worked at Piggotts sweet factory in Cross Street, or at East Sussex Growers at Dittons Corner. My wife worked at Maynards cafe in the High Street.

Principal families in Brook Street were the Dells, Sands and the Parsons. I think there was a dairy and a radio shop at the top end of Brook Street. We cannot agree about the High Street shops. The dairy was I believe Wood's and the radio shop Hailsham Radio. In the lane opposite Cross Street was a carpenters, half way down was Pharoah Plant Hire (the new house). Local milk man was Mr Wood, he used a Mini van and came very early in the morning. George Townsend was the local scrap man and he came every Saturday morning - he would ring a large hand bell. He had a large cream and red Austin lorry and sold logs in the winter - 2/6 a bag or 10/- for five.

Our local doctor was Morgan who lived in Old Drive and had

his surgery in the High Street. His surgery waiting room had brown lino on the floor and an old gas fire. I don't think he had two chairs the same. Over his examination couch he had a large picture of an early Lister operation, he was an old Army doctor I believe.

Local school was the old building, now gone, on the right of School Lane and Miss Trip was the teacher for the first year infants. The single carriage train, Jenny, still ran to Hailsham at this time - I think a lot of Polegate children went to the senior school there.

All crossings down the back lanes were manned with a cottage for the keeper. These were closed at night and if you came back late at night you had to get the keeper to open them. There was a cottage and I think strawberry fields as what is now Guardian Court and a large house behind the council houses in Hailsham Road. I can remember two large iron gates and a long drive.

There was a derelict laundry in St Leonard's Terrace. We had a village carnival in early June, followed by a village fete, stands, stalls and sideshows. We also had a steam engine rally down the Lewes Road. This was organised by Arthur Hanmoore who was the local Pearl Insurance agent.

Of the local pubs the Junction was run by landlady who's name I cannot remember. It was a spit and sawdust pub, even the saloon bar was full of really tatty old furniture. The Dinkum was called the Polegate Inn, with the door in the front in High Street. The landlord was I believe from Rhodesia and his name was Cecil. I remember some tradition about the gas lamp over the fireplace being lit during the opening hours. The name Dinkum comes from Australian troops expression fair dinkum (good). What is now the Co-Op block was some cottages, a coal wharf and Scats Feed Mill. I think there was some railway sidings and a goods yard for freight and parcels.

Polegate had two garages at this time. Waghorn's Service Station, now AutoWise by the Horse & Groom, and Polegate Motors - now the Tesco complex. A Mr Petch owned Polegate Motors and he lived in an Island Close house on the Hailsham Road. They had an Austin-Morris franchise, both repairs if required. Both garages sold petrol, paraffin and oil and some parts. I can remember a fuss, I think it was in the late 1960s, about the loss of the local Liberty Stone from the High Street. The developers took it away and dumped it in a gravel pit. Old people speak of a tin hut at the now site of the Community Centre, used as a dance hall by the local youth. I am also told that the Junction pub hall was used for school dinners by the children.

Bill Hill, Polegate, July 2004.

EIGHT YEARS IN TOWN

Our first day in Polegate was a bright February morning. Just right for a walk through Polly Arch (ever muddy) to find an open community field just right for a good walk even though the grass did need a good cut. We walked around the field to the meadow at the top which we entered via a lovely green path. This beautiful path soon became a horrible and rough track which was made from old rubbish dumped by big lorries. This track was not really used as it was not safe.

Old Polegate station was a restaurant - not bad, but now it is owned as Buddies and is very good. The Post Office was on the corner of the High Street with a nice little shop, which has now moved to the Co-op. There was also two hardware shops, two carpet shops and lovely shop that sold everything from socks, gloves, slippers and Wellingtons. About seven years ago a lovely art shop came to town, but it soon disappeared.

Polegate also had a big car park with four little gardens which were lovely in the spring. Now there is only a small car park with no flowering shrubs, one hardware shop, one carpet shop and no little shop with everything for sale. We have a lovely patchwork shop and a good Internet cafe and our florist which sells some beautiful flowers.

Pamela Fry, Polegate, May 2003.

LOOKING BACK

During my childhood the fox hounds would meet at the Horse & Groom every Saturday during the hunting season. Many folk living in Polegate would turn out to see the hounds meet and take the traditional drink before the hunt started. The horse trough is still to be seen outside the Horse & Groom, although it is now used to grow flowers in.

These were the years when Caleb Diplock was known as the Mayor of Polegate. Mr Diplock was very wealthy and was the owner of several public houses in Eastbourne, as well as being the owner of the Eastbourne Gas Company. He lived in a lovely big house opposite St John's Church which was entered from a wide drive with a stag statue at the entrance and this statue is still to be seen on a stand in the grounds of the Bernhard Baron Homes which were built on ground that Mr Diplock owned and where he had allowed horse and pony racing to take place.

He was quite a generous person and gave a lot of money to the village of Polegate, including funds to help build St John's Church. His image can be seen in the stained glass window above the altar where his face is shown on the left-hand side as one of Christ's disciples. At Christmas he would walk around the village and on meeting any children he would give them a sixpence and some of these children would then run ahead and make sure they met him again so that they got another sixpence!

Caleb Diplock owned Diplock's Wood in Wannock Road and he would often give parties for the people of Polegate, when food and tea urns would be brought from Southdown Hall by servants in horse and traps. His large household gave employment to many local people, including my elder sisters who after leaving school went to work at Diplock's Hall as scullery maids and working their way up to become cooks or ladies maids. Every Sunday Mr Diplock and his sister Sarah would attend church and Miss Diplock would sweep into the church just before the service started wearing a long dress and coat and hat all made from the best material available, in the winter she always had her hands tucked into a fir muff.

When Caleb Diplock junior died he left much of his money to charities and good causes, but due to something wrong with the wording of his will some distant relations from Australia put in a claim for his wealth. When they won the Court case benefactors had to give all the money back. The old house and land was sold.

At the top end of the high street was a laundry which was run by a Polegate man to make work for local people. Next door to this was an undertakers, then there was small butchers shop and a sweet shop which was run by Dusty Miller and a Post Office, then next came the Chapel building. On the opposite side of the road there was playing field which is now covered by houses and the later Post Office.

In 1916 Dittons Wood used to be covered with primroses and bluebells in the spring and with the many shady oak trees it was a favourite place for people from Eastbourne to take their children out for a day picking flowers, bird nesting or having a picnic. The woodland belonged to the Duke of Devonshire who put a gate for people to get in for free. A Mr Dickson had a nursery garden in Pevensey Road from which he supplied flowers and vegetables to the local area. There was a large railway shunting yard for the trucks of coal and food which came by rail everyday and this area ran from Polegate railway station to the Polly Arch bridge in Pevensey Road.

There were no buildings along the Pevensey Road and the first house to be built there was called Cranlea due to its owner, Jesse Mann, having connections with Cranleigh in Surrey. The house has since been pulled down and another built on the site. A short time later Gilbert Levett built some bungalows along Pevensey Road and he called them Nursery Close and then he went on to build Fellands, 25 Pevensey Road, where he and his wife lived for the rest of their lives. Gradually he built houses and bungalows all along one side of Pevensey Road which had been Duke of Devonshire's land. Levett's only stopped building when WWII started in 1939. During the 1950s he built the Levett estate of bungalows on the fields which throughout the war had been farmed by him, as well as containing a sawmill from which he helped to keep the home fires burning by supplying firewood and logs.

The fields the other side of Pevensey Road were then used as allotments for the people of Polegate, Harold Gates of Station Road had his coal depot there for many years. These fields were also a playground for children until they were built upon in the 1970s. It is said that until the late 1920s Pevensey Road - once it passed Dittons Corner - was merely a dirt track that eventually met up with the Eastbourne to Hailsham Road at Stone Cross.

One of the landmarks at Polegate for more than century was the old Granary or Catt's Mill which was owned and run by Mr Catt. He was chubby little fellow with rosy cheeks who was always very cheerful and could be a bit saucy to the ladies. Mr Catt could easily carry a sack of corn, which weighed two hundred and fifty pounds, on his shoulder - although he was quite bandy-legged and perhaps that is why! The following report appeared in the local paper in the 1960s . . . a landmark of Polegate for more than century, the old granary at the rail goods yard, disappeared yesterday as the empty shell went up in smoke. Demolition contractor Mr Bernard Best burnt out the remaining timbers and set to work knocking down the walls.

The station centrepiece

British Rail were able to move the station back to its original site when the Hailsham line closed in the 1960's. The local press reported . . . the final blow of the Beeching axe on all that remains of the picturesque Cuckoo Line fell when the 10.30pm train left Hailsham for Polegate. Many rail enthusiasts were expected to make the three mile trip down the single track to Polegate from the growing town of Hailsham that will loose its passenger service. Hailsham Rural District Council fought the closure tooth and nail and urging anyone suffering hardship to pressure the authorities. Noting that problems of Sunday travel and infrequency of bus routes. Near the Granary was an open space called the Dock, where lorries assembled to collect sacks of corn. This was also here the racing horses were loaded and unloaded and walked through the fields by Railway Terrace into Station Road to be put into horse boxes. This was quite a spectacle for local children.

Corrie Taylor used to hold a fair in front of the Church of England School in Hailsham Road. A bright maypole was erected for children to dance around holding colourful ribbons and toffee apples were handed to the youngsters. Local children helped out by playing the piano and parents had to pay three pence to get in for the evening. Corrie Taylor's house at the top of the High Street changed to be Polegate laundry, employing about four local people. The Dinkum was run by John Colbran and his wife Hope Still Colbran and consisted of one bar where sawdust covered the floor and it had wooden benches to sit upon. The bottle and jug was on the north side, where children were sent to get a jug of ale for their parents. Nearby was a small garage run by a Mr Fowler and a blacksmith where horses were shod.

Black Path was small lane which runs alongside the railway leading from the High Street to a tunnel underneath the old Polegate Station. This led out into Station Road and was used a short cut from the village to the station. On one side were railway allotments and on the other side fields that were very dark and creepy at night, although many courting couples made good use of them.

There were no street lights in Polegate until gas arrived, this was thought wonderful when installed in homes to replace the old and smelly oil lamps. Mr Fowler used to go around at 9 o'clock every night and put the gas street lights on. While father was working in the Polegate Station signal box we lived in Railway Terrace and he only had to walk up the garden path and would be indoors. My five brothers all worked for Southern Railway after leaving school.

Compiled from notes written by Edith Levett that were found after her demise in 1999 at the age of ninety years. She had lived in Polegate throughout her life.

POLEGATE TREACLE MINES

Folklore tales abound regarding the Polegate Treacle Mines - possibly perpetuated by the local confectionery industry. However newspaper correspondence in 1983 prompted several intriguing accounts - or was it just another April Fool idea?

I write with reference to the Eastbourne Post article regarding Polegate Treacle Mines. I am a model railway enthusiast and have constructed a model based on the Cuckmere Valley Railway and Polegate Treacle Mines Railway.

My idea is the P.T.M. Railway was constructed to transport the treacle from the mines to Willingdon Harbour and Wannock Quay, where it was put on barges which went down the Wannock canal to Cuckmere Haven. However silting up of the canal caused the mines company to construct a railway from Willingdon to Wannock, through Wilmington to Alfriston and the Cuckmere Valley Railway where the ore was shipped to the Continent. A line was constructed later to Polegate Junction, so the ore could be sent by rail all over Britain. All of these lines were built to narrow gauge standard.

My layout shows the line from Wannock Quay, through Wilmington to the Alfriston works depot. My model layout has been exhibited at a couple of exhibitions run by Eastbourne Railway Society. I am hoping in the future to assemble a history of the Cuckmere Valley Railway and Polegate Treacle Mines Railway and its associations with treacle mining in Polegate.

Ian James, Eastbourne, April 1983.

WELL, WELL, WELL!

Those of us who have lived in Polegate a long time are familiar with the stories put about concerning the Polegate Treacle Mine. To get at a Polegatian you only had to ask . . . how production was going at the Mines? or . . . have they let you out for the day? The product of the mines was said to be shipped out from Wannock Docks. These stories were regulars on the stage. Variety artistes, concert parties, and pantomime comedians made regular references to poor old Polegate and the mines as if it was the world's end. The jokes were taken up around the town by those wishing to taunt the country hicks.

Were these stories dreamt up in the minds of then entertainers just as leg-pulls, or were they playing more seriously on the credulity of their audiences who would know better? Or did they circulate anyway amongst the artisans of Eastbourne, who with their parents, had come into the growing town from surrounding countryside? Polegate and Wannock were small insignificant country hamlets - Polegate began to grow in the 1860s with the pace accelerating in the 1930s, when Wannock too began to grow. Or did the story start at our end - to boast about something the townees do not have?

Several decades ago the West Sussex Gazette tried to solve the mystery of the mines, as they are said to exist in West Sussex also - at Sompting, Burpham, Patcham, and Rowhook. Further afield there were famous mines at Chobham, Surrey, where again there were Docks. Macclesfield, Cheshire, Trelleck, Monmouth, Oxshott and Claygate, Surrey, also claimed the the presence of treacle mines, and maybe there are others.

Jacqueline Simpson, author of a book on Sussex superstitions, wrote to the newspaper that she could not date the origin and rise of the leg-pull. In her opinion to say that someone worked in the treacle mines was to imply that they were lazy and did not work, and that a later use of the phrase 'going on the treacle' meant drawing the National Assistance.

No dates are quoted in this and Jacqueline Simpson wondered and if Lewis Carroll was responsible for the invention. His Alice in Wonderland was first published in 1865. At the Mad Hatter's Tea Party the Doormouse related the story of Elsie, Lacie and Tillie and they lived at the bottom of a well . . . it was a treacle mine. Although Carroll was not the first popular author in the nonsense field, his Alice stories were bestsellers. Had Lewis Carroll heard of treacle wells and mines as folk traditions? Or was he the true inventor of the story which took root in various locations?

Another suggestion is made - for nearly seventy years brickfields existed in various parts of Polegate. The pug prepared from the clay for brick, tiles and pottery making, was a sticky, clinging, semi-liquid ooze. Who amongst those who work on clay sites doesn't know how one's boots get trapped - lift your feet and half a hundredweight of clay comes too!

This wet clay creeps everywhere. A lot of Polegate's roads were not made up until after the 1939-1945 war and when we used to play around the village we could get slubbed up to the eyebrows very quickly. Yellow mud all over the place. No wonder it could be called treacle.

Vera Hodsoll, Polegate, May 1994.

A STICKY WICKET TALE

Cricket in the early days was played in a paddock in which there was a large shed, kindly loaned by a local farmer. A special Saturday afternoon match was arranged between locals and townees. Two local characters were detailed to clean the shed and clear the pitch where moles had been very active. Armed with shovels, scythes and besoms, they set of on a cart hauled by two donkeys and were soon busy at work. The weather had been kind for days and the granular clay heavies were easy to shovel up into the cart and the grass beneath swept to remove the remaining dusty stuff.

Bill and Tom were nearly finished, but a sudden thunderstorm and heavy rain put paid to outside work. The two donkeys didn't think much of it and they played up something rotten. With the mules settled and tethered the two worthies set to and cleaned up the shed (pavilion). The day of the match dawned with clear sky, bright sunshine and a nice drying breeze. This permitted the task to be completed, the match to be played and watched in ideal conditions.

The local team won and all adjourned to the pavilion to enjoy the free local brewed ale. Bill and Tom where in jocular spirits and began talking of the cleaning up job . . .

Bill: Those little gents had been real busy hadn't they.
Tom: Yes, I bet their black and velvet coats got in a mess.
Bill: Reckon the tunnels get a bit sticky.
Tom: Jest like syrup I'd say.
Bill: Wonder how deep they go?
Tom: Not very, else they'd never get the stuff to the surface.
Bill: Wonder how many there are, don't see much of them?
Tom: No, only where they've been.
Bill: Them ol' asses can be awkward to handle.
Tom: Yes, I'd export them.
A stranger had overheard this conversation and was mystified. He thought, little men in tunnels, sticky, like syrup, molasses. Overcome by his curiosity he spoke to the two old sticks and asked incredulously . . . were you speaking of a treacle mine? Yes said Bill, didn't you know about it?

Yours (not) sincerely A.N.Parks

OUR TIME AT 14 HIGH STREET

Trading as Buckley's in the High Street our time in Polegate from 1976-1986 brings back many happy memories, not the least Brian serenading our customers with his dulcet tones. This was not always appreciated by everyone and one burly gentleman, who used to call regularly for his early morning papers, would often pick up half a dozen rubber balls from a roundel near the door and throw them at Brian to stop his singing!

From a 1983 window display of housekeeping memorabilia, which won a national competition, a small museum was created in the basement, which like Topsy, grew and grew. Within three years the collection out grew the premises and is now housed in Battle under the name of Yesterday's World.

Annette Buckley, June 2004.

ORCHARDLEIGH FAMILY HOME

Our family home at 18 St John's Road was built in 1935 and has been in the family for generations, my great grandfather brought the property for his mistress! It used to have a big plot of land alongside, but grandfather sold most of it for £300 and now three bungalows have been built there.

The house was called Orchardleigh because there used to be so many trees in the grounds, including apple, plum and damson. The three bedroomed house is built in traditional Sussex tile-hung style with a lovely oak front door. The staircase and internal doors are also in oak. The house used to be neighbours with Redlands that has been derelict for many years now is to be re-developed. That plot was owned by the chap who lives next door and he has tried to get permission for all sorts of developments!

Gemma Cater, May 1998.

SCOUTING FOR BOYS

Tent pegging and decorated bicycle competitions, sideshows and stalls are among the attractions of Polegate Scout group's Scouterama held at the junior School. The purpose being to raise funds to equip a new patrol and for expenses for Cubs' functions, said Scoutmaster J. White.

More help with training is needed together with a place of their own to meet as they have a waiting list of boys wishing to join.

Clive Page, Polegate Diary, June 1965.

HOW THE WEST WAS WON - AT POLEGATE

There is something Dodgy about Polegate, a no-account town that is spread across the flatlands around the railroad halt and the intersection of the highway to the west and the old north-south trail. Deceptively English in character, with its High Street shops and bungalow estates, Polegate could be an illusion, an elaborate facsimile of suburban Sussex. The real hidden Polegate is obviously an outpost of the Old West - otherwise how can you explain the plethora of cowboy books written within the purlieus? They so magnificently capture the essence of brutal life on the old-time frontier that it is impossible to believe the author(s) live(s) in Polegate.

Now the suspicion is that the two Polegate authors who have Westerns out - John Dyson and Wolf Lundgren - are actually the same person. Maybe he (or she) also writes under a dozen more pen names, all of them resident in Polegate. Only the publisher knows, but it would be a shame to enquire and ruin the picture of a posse of crusty old timers meeting on a shady timber boardwalk outside the saloon to reminisce about the glory days, have a bit of a spit and map out their next plots.

Dyson's twenty-second Western, The Horsehead Trail, is about Charlie Goodnight, who leaves the Texas Rangers and sets out to raise enough money to marry Mary Ann . . . the sweetest li'l chickadee I ever set my eyes upon. Charlie has a herd of longhorns to sell and instead of driving his beasts north to the Kansas cow towns. He heads south west into Comanche country, blazing a trail across hundreds of miles of desert. Charlie Goodnight the man who blazed the Horsehead Trail died aged 93 in 1929, sixty three years after his epic journey. He left a town, a college and a legend in his name.

Lundgren's book The Renos tells a true story of five railroad robbing Reno brothers, the scourge of Indiana and Missouri in the mid 19th century. The Pinkertons were hot on their trail when a railroad guard was gunned down and murdered by the brothers, proud of their never having killed, were branded murders. Both books (were) available from Black Horse Westerns from Robert Hale Co.

Sussex Express Book Reviews, July 1991.

RESPECTED REMINISCENCES

I remember the bakehouse and sweet factory in Polegate and the brickyards in Brook Street, Andrew's brickyard was near Nelson Terrace (Hailsham Road). Victoria and Albert Roads were cart tracks. In the High Street there was a blacksmiths, north of where the Dinkum is now. Alongside the roadway in Gilda Crescent were swamps with willow trees. These were cut down periodically and the wood sent to Kent for cricket bats. There were about eight shops, a large laundry stood on the corner where a nursery is now. In Station Road at the top of the High Street was the Toll House. There was a little fire station in Victoria Road manned by volunteers, local lads.

Old Drive was the entrance to Southdown Hall, the home of Caleb Diplock, known as the squire of Polegate. He owned a large part of the village. There was a lake in the grounds with goldfish as big as herrings. Halfway along the drive was a brick archway with a stag on top. The stag is now in the grounds of Bernhard Baron Homes and can be seen from the Lewes Road. Bernhard Baron Homes was built by Diplock. When he died he left his money to charity, but a relative in Australia who came over and contested the will got everything including money already paid to charity.

Until just after WWII the windmill still ground its corn. The sweeps rotted so Mr Ovenden, the miller, installed electricity. After his death the mill stood empty until being restored by the preservation people. The watermill also ground corn, stood near the windmill, the owner's daughter built a house with it. Park Croft was the fever hospital, scarlet fever for the district. Patients were transported by horse ambulance. The first bus was run by Mr Henry Twine, from Jevington to Eastbourne eight pennies return, a motor bus.

There was a marshalling yard at the junction, working day and night and very noisy. London trains, one half came from Hastings, one from Eastbourne, and they were joined at Polegate for London. On return from London when the train reached Wootton bridge the train was slipped. The guard in the middle of the train disconnected the two halves. The front picked up speed, the back had enough momentum to bring it back into the station and stop. Sometimes it stopped halfway across the crossing.

There was always happenings of interest. Every year there was a torchlight procession with 1,000 torches in November. Fancy dress, floats, very large bonfire and big firework display. Lewes bonfire societies used to help, so we held ours a day late then we helped them on the 5th. There was always a Father Christmas, my father Old Sam was the original Father Christmas. On Christmas Eve he visited the poor and took the children toys from his own pocket. When he died his son took over as Polegate's Father Christmas - one year he had to play Father Christmas eight times. He doesn't charge, just asks for transport unless it is somewhere he can go by bus.

From the railway goods yard coal was transported to Friston Waterworks, delivered by a team of four horses and wagons. Wannock Gardens were over 100 years old, beautiful old mill gardens were on the opposite corner with the watermill and a bakery, they ground their own flour. The Wannock Glen was very beautiful, they built a pathway along. In the middle of the glen was a bridge with huts on it where they held Sunday afternoon tea dances for 1/6d.

Sledging took place on Good Friday on the grassy Downs. Practically every child in the village would go up to 'Donkey Oller'. If you returned with backside of your trousers intact, then you hadn't been sledging - boy or girl. There were at times steam roundabouts in the brickyard, swing boats, hula hoop stalls, pony rides. Also there were gala days with fancy dress processions in the field opposite where the library is now.

Sam Richardson, interviewed in December 1982.

SOME GOOD OLD DAYS.

It was all so different in the 1940's, 1950's, 1960's. Polegate was a small village where everyone seemed to know everyone and a walk to the village could take hours because of the number of people one would meet. Passing the time of day and comments about the weather were always the main topics of conversation - followed by any gossip going the rounds. The roads where cyclists could wobble along without fear were quiet as there were very few private cars or taxis, delivery lorries very few as great use was made of the railway. Most goods came via the trains, including papers and the post which a postman would collect on his bike. They would take post to Polegate GPO Sorting Office and it was delivered the same day that it was received.

The railway station was so clean and the people who worked there took great pride in keeping it that way, one did not dare drop a piece of paper onto the platform. The refreshment room was cosy and warm and the water boiler for making the hot drinks was brass, it was cleaned and polished every day so you could see your reflection in it - there were pure white lace curtains at every window. Porters would open doors for the ladies to get in and out of trains and they would know everything about the train times and they would carry luggage to guard vans.

Porters were responsible for the carrier pigeons which would arrive in a basket from all parts of the country, porters would have to let them go out at certain times. I often went to the station to watch them being let out, being fascinated by the way they circled around for a while and then went off homewards. Most nights there would be shunting of the numerous railway trucks which arrived throughout the daytime and this noise would sometimes go on for most of the night. We became used to it and invariably slept through it, when the shunting stopped my parents could not sleep for a while as they missed the noise.

One thing most children enjoyed was collecting car numbers and putting them in to a notebook. Polegate crossroads was the best place for this and I would sit there for hours to get one or two numbers in my book. When there were a several of us collecting numbers there would be great excitement each time a car or lorry appeared. The school in Hailsham Road was the Infants School for children aged five years to seven years of age. After a few weeks there I was walking home alone as every child in the village went to the school and there was always someone to walk home with. After school we would go out to play in friends garden, or sometimes the girls would play hopscotch on the path if we could find any chalk to mark out a pitch, while the while the boys would kick a ball about. There were no school dinners when I first started school and we had to take a sandwich and a drink if we lived too far away from the school to walk home and back in the lunch hour.

During the war when there was a build-up for the invasion of France there were many convoys of lorries passing through Polegate. These mainly carried American and Canadian soldiers and we would rush to wave to the soldiers and sometimes they would throw us some chewing gum or sweets. This was all so wonderful as sweets were rationed and we only got a couple of ounces per week, we would gobble up sweets that we managed to catch.

There were certain 'ladies' who were always around when the convoys stopped and I remember hearing my mother commenting upon the nylon stockings some people seemed to have plenty of. I wondered why she didn't come out to see the soldiers, as I had seen stockings being handed out!

My father was doing WD work during the war and he would come home covered in dust and dirt and the conversation would be quietly conducted regarding amounts of damage and casualties, but my parents often looked very sad so I knew something awful had happened. The bombing of the Southlands estate was one of the occasions when father was out for hours trying to help and he was really shocked by what he had seen when he returned.

Good old days.

Jeanne Fry, nee Levett, July 2004.

POLEGATE AT THE BEGINNING OF THE 1900s.

Written by Louisa Jane Blackwell, September in 1956, aged 80 years.
With additions by her eldest son Frank Charles Blackwell in 1976, in his 80th year. All via Ron Levett.

Some memories that have survived through all the 80 years of my life . . .

I was born at Lower Willingdon in 1872 and there spent the next six years. I do not know at what age I started school at Upper Willingdon, a mile's walk each day. A little band of us children all went together. For Sunday School I used to go to a little isolated chapel round a country lane. My memory of that is a bit hazy, but about the day school there are sonic things that stand out as clear and fresh as ever.

One was the mulberry tree, the branches of which used to hang well over the garden wall and the grass verge beneath. There was always a race to see which could get there first and so get the pick of the fallen fruit when its season came round, no-one ever said us nay.

Then a little further on we used to go up some wooden steps in the roadside bank, over a low stile and across a cornfield. At least it was not always that, there were times when it had been fresh ploughed and the path had to be re-made once more. Travelling was anything but a joy and pleasure then with our small feet, but as it was used quite a lot we soon had other help. That brought us to another stile into a large green field, which landed us safely into the road where the school stood.

On the other side of the big entrance gate was a bit of ground surrounded by rather high flint walls with a large gate opening onto the road. That they told me was called a pound where all the cattle found straying on the mud were confined until the owner claimed them. I think they had to pay a certain sum of money before they were released, that I think was under the control of the village policeman.

Then, another little incident of my first school days still stays green in my memory. We little tots always had to sit on a sort of gallery, a set of steps or stairs rising one above the other. I did not stay there long enough to get a promotion to a better seat. Then one memorable day the teacher dealt out some small pieces of material, we were to learn how to sew. She then came around with a box of tiny thimbles and fitted each of one of us with. It was not very long before mine went hurling across the room with the cry . . . I can't keep that silly ole thing on my finger. In later years I was top of my class for needlework, but more of that later.

Just below where I lived was the village horse pond and I used to love to watch the teams of horses on their way home from ploughing etc, hot and thirsty, go in for a nice refreshing drink. I am not clear about this, but I think they used to go in on side and come out on the other as it seemed to be very shallow at the road or entrance end.

Then there is one other memory of those early days I would like to mention for it has lived in my memory so very clear through all the intervening years. After my parents moved to Polegate that left my grandmother quite alone and I think she thought a good deal of me judging by after events. I had probably been spending a few days with her, then she decided to take me back home on the next morrow. I think early to bed and early to rise was the idea

Just whatever would people think if ever we met anyone, but grandmother's word was law and not even tears would make her relent. I just had to do as I was told and no nonsense. Then she said we had best walk on the side of the road where it was a bit rough and uneven to avoid slipping, rather like remaking a path through the ploughed field. But all went well on our journey, she delivered the goods (which was me) all safe and sound.

I have often wondered why we could not have waited till later in the day when travelling might have been better, but the old lady had had a pretty hard and strenuous life as grandfather was bedridden for some years, thus making her a typical old won't be druv sort. If she set out to do anything, well she just did it.

Now starts my new life in Polegate from the age of six . . .

My grandmother always looked well after me and made and provided the whole of my clothes. She was a splendid needle worker like the majority of old folks in those days. I can just remember a white frock of all hand made embroidery; there was quite a lot of it done then. She was always talking of making me a tuskin? Hat or bonnet, whatever it might be, but she never found the time for which I was very thankful. I naturally wanted to be dressed like other girls, not to have to wear something at which they would have laughed.

Growing up quickly

How well do I remember that day when she brought me my first pair of boned corsets . . . come on girl, it's about time we began to think about your figure. So into harness I had to go and did she pull those laces tight, I could hardly breathe. All the sympathy I got from her was . . . I don't care, you have just got to come to them so there. You'll soon get used to them. Which I suppose I did after easing the laces a bit.

It was grandmother who bought me the only two dolls I ever had. One doll cost 6/4d and the other 33/4d, but they were great treasures for all that poor mother never seemed to have any money to spare for toys etc. I may have had an occasional farthing or halfpenny for sweets, but very occasionally indeed. What a vast difference to children present day spending when even a sixpence is looked upon with scorn oftimes.

Thus gran kept bringing along something or other new for me until one day she brought a piece of cheap material . . . now my girl, you are old enough now to start making your own. My first attempt was a princess robe, as they were then called. The kitchen table was not big enough to cut it out on, so I laid it on the floor and managed to make something of it that way. The only fault with it seemed to be rather too pointed at the seams. Still I lived and learned and later got quite a good hand at making my own frocks, or dresses as we called them then.

On looking back I owe quite a bit to old gran. She died at the age of 87 years just after I was married. One would always find her busy making patched quilts as long as she could ply a needle.

Her ambition was to make one for each of her grand-daughters, but I afraid she did not accomplish the task, not even the first one. I don't think either I, or my cousins, were at all disappointed. I forgot to say she was my father's mother. There were three boys in all and what a struggle it must have been to bring them up with never a penny coming in from poor old grandfather to help since he was unable to work for years.

My home for twenty-seven years

In 1878 Brook Street consisted of a grocers shop on one corner of Cross Street and a baker and sweet shop on the other from which ran a row of twenty cottages, that was on the right hand side as entered from the main road. At the bottom was a little meadow with a large clump of fir trees at the back. A blackberry hedge stood in front with a fair size brickyard the far end. On the left hand side were two cottages then an entrance to a slaughter house and Mr Tolhurst's stables, as I think he kept several horses for his van work. Then my father bought the next two or three plots and had two five-bedroomed cottages built. Beyond that was just the garden of the cottages opposite with a small green meadow at the end.

At the top of Brook Street was a clump of willows and just a two rail fence in front, but that seemed to be the dumping ground for everybody's old junk for it was a most untidy, disreputable place imaginable. At the bottom of our garden was a fairly wide ditch. which often in winter time over flowed and came more than halfway up our garden path. It is no doubt that is what gave the name Brook Street. Before it reached the main road and railways it entered a sort of culvert coming out somewhere in the fields beyond, where I think it was joined by another from Wannock Glen.

For many years, even after several more houses were built, the road was in a terrible state. One or two places had old railway sleepers laid to provide a crossing in winter. All day long one horse carts were going to and fro from the brickyard, churning the mud to a morass. I have seen the poor horses fall into the worst and deepest places and with a load of bricks behind them it was no easy task to get them on their feet again.

I can remember the original railway station with its tarmac platforms and brief canopy over the waiting rooms, sometime going to and fro to Eastbourne or Hailsham in those days, although I could not have been very old at the time. The stationmaster was Mr Gladwin who lived right on the platform down side. The Railway Hotel was and still is on the opposite side (Junction Hotel), both of these were used as the Post Office for some little time. There was also the signalman's cottage near the gates facing the signal box, but that was pulled down many years ago. I think it was more timber than bricks as I remember it.

Then from the signal box followed Mr Diplock's field where cricket matches, flower shows and all gala days were held. Just over the fence from the road was a bank with large shady trees and a most suitable field for the purpose in every way. At the far end were three cottages, the policeman living in the centre one. Previously he had occupied No 1 Brook Street joining the baker's shop, but as there were two houses above the grocer's on the right hand side it might perhaps have started as No 3.

Village processions

To return to the three cottages opposite the church, adjoining them was the shop of the village. Leastways for us children for it sold toys, amongst newspapers and other miscellaneous articles. Never an evening passed, and often during the day out of school hours, did we have to go down to Waghorn's to see if there had been anything fresh placed in the window. I think they sold sweets and ginger pop.

Then just a little walk further on there was the entrance to Southdown Hall where lived the only moneyed gentleman that Polegate could boast of. No procession, whatever it was for, ever failed to turn in there and that was our chance of getting in close proximity to the front of the house since it could not be seen from the roadway, always high hedges and trees to hide it from view. He certainly proved a true and helpful friend to me afterwards in giving me nice books that he thought would help me in the Christian life. He left Polegate a short time later, all much to my sorrow for truly I had lost a friend.

A little time later the Congregational Hall was built (1904) and, with my girlfriend at that time, we both went over to that. Sankey's hymns were sung and the services were ever bright and helpful. I had some very happy times in that little building and was a Sunday School teacher for over four years. On the Sunday before I was married I was presented with a lovely family bible. Three of my children were baptised there and the fourth was the first child to be baptised in the new building that left our little corrugated iron one in the background. I shall always love it for its crowds of happy memories.

School days

Then we come to what is now the infants school, but until the new one was built (junction of School Lane and Station Road) it took the whole of the Polegate children. In my day we had to pass seven standards, when we reached that goal we were quite free to leave school. I accomplished it at the age of eleven and was able to say goodbye to school just a month after that birthday. There used to be one big gruelling day a year when the Inspector came and we had our big examination. What long hours we seemed to have to sit for it, not one scholar dared be absent on that all-important day. We were supplied with large sheets of paper and pens and not a sound or whisper was heard beyond instructions given by the great man of the day.

One year I remember a girl being brought to the school with a big shawl round her. Less than a fortnight later we followed her to her grave, she was eleven years old. Better she had stayed at home on examination day, but every scholar was so anxious to pass.

Somehow school days were not such a pleasure, as they seem to be now. I have seen mothers chasing their boys round Davis Field (corner of Station Road and top of High Street) with a stick to drive them to school. The old attendance officer pretty often had to make a call at the homes to know why such and such a child was not at school on a certain day or days. Mostly mothers thought that they were at school.

We always had to take two pence on a Monday morning for our school money. Times were far harder for the working class in those days for wages were very low and no work meant no money at all coming in. No government help in those good or bad old days, yet folks were far more contented then than ever they are today.

As one of the older girls I, with two or three others, used to stay and sweep and dust the school after 4 o'clock for which we were paid 1/6d a week. Not a lot when shared out, but we were well satisfied. During the winter, when it got dark so early, we had to put a spurt on as there was no light available beyond what came through the window on just one side of the room. On Friday nights we left it over till Saturday so that was always a glad night. I cannot describe the quantity of thick dust we had to contend with on those rough floorboards of the big room, then all the dusting to follow. Yes, I think we earned our pay. Two of those girls with whom I worked were still living in September 1956 aged 86 years and 88 years. Whenever we have met we have had many a laugh over our school days.

Adjoining the school was a great meadow with a little shawl or coppice on the road side as far as the turning that is now Albert Road I think. Nothing more for some years till one reached Bay Cottage. Near there was an old green lane where we used to pick primroses and blackberries in their season. Beyond that there were two small coppices where bluebells grew on side of the road, then all the fields as far as Cophall Farm. From the laundry corner on the other side of the school or Hailsham Road was just fields and high hedges with two cottages and another standing endways to the road at the turning to Sayerlands. On that road it was quite a long walk to where one came to two more cottages and nearby an old thatched one. Farther on towards the railway lines and gates was Sayerlands House, a gentleman's residence. It was there that we always went for our school treats, the younger ones conveyed in farm wagons.

There is a brass plate near the font in Polegate Church, which for me holds rather tender and sacred memories. There was to be a confirmation in Hailsham Church in May 1888. The Rev. William Groves had managed to find around fourteen or fifteen candidates for it when I presented myself at the first class unasked or invited. Perhaps I was not considered good enough, anyway, I felt the slight.

I don't think that anyone under the age of 15 was confirmed in those days. The Reverend continued to let all the rest pass through the door with a handshake and a kindly word and then he closed the door and gave me a very serious talking to. As if he thought I was only doing it for a bit of fun. Had he but known it there was not one amongst that little band in more deadly earnest than I and so I carried on with the rest of them. Then the great day arrived, but, alas, only a few days earlier our beloved pastor was called away through the accidental drowning of a brother, as recorded on the brass plate. The thing that touched me on the morning of the confirmation was the arrival of a black edged letter and a very nice letter it was. I never knew if the others received one as well, but that he should think of me at any rate in the midst of his deep sorrow. I have kept and treasured that letter all through.

A bigger village

In the meantime houses had sprung up everywhere like a field of mushrooms. The two derelict buildings were finished off finally, one opened as an eating house (we never called it a restaurant). It was first in the charge of an elderly spinster and her aged mother. I think she was noted for her 2d meat pies, and they were not very small either. By taking a plate one could get a nice helping of hot roast beef or mutton for the small sum of 3d - there was always something tempting and nice in the window.

The next shop to it was the village Post Office for some little time, until the present one was built and taken over. Talking of the Post Office reminds me of the old milkman back in my school days who used to ply between Eastbourne and Cross-in-Hand to collect all the mail bags as he passed through. So punctual was he at 8 o'clock every night when he used to blow a bugle or horn of some sort that folks could set their clocks by him. How many times have I heard my mother say . . . there goes the mail man, off to bed you go. I think he had to find his own horse and cart, first an ordinary square market cart, hence he could if he wished carry passengers. An aunt of mine once told me how she and my mother met him at 6 o'clock (am) from near his starting point and rode with him to Upper Willingdon where they had a married brother living. They were again picked up in the evening for the return journey. My aunt said at some of the places he called at the mailbags were lowered into the cart from bedroom windows. That brings yet another link with the past to my mind.

Travelling around

After I was married every Tuesday and Friday a country carrier used to travel from East Hoathley onto Eastbourne. He drove a covered mail van with a wooden form on either side for the accommodation of any passengers desiring to travel that way. True we could board it at the top of Brook Street and thus save the walk to the station, but one did have to be in any hurry to reach their destination. For one thing the old horse travelled at a very leisurely pace, perhaps he was getting tired by the time he reached Polegate.

At intervals one would come across a little piece of white flag fluttering from a gateway which was to say would the carrier please call, a parcel or some laundry perhaps to go. I am afraid he was a bit of a gossip, for he seemed absent for quite along time at some of the houses. Then eventually we jogged on a little further, finally landing near Eastbourne Station to spend what was left of our day. If we wished to return in the same way we had to wait at a given spot. I think most folks preferred to patronise the railway as a speedier return home.

I well remember the building of Polegate's second train station, though not very old at the time. I like to think I had a hand in it as I often used to go with a pal taking her father's dinner every day, he was one of the workmen. The old black path as it was called was not very well liked at first. It seemed a rather long monotonous walk with nothing but a tarred wooden fence on the footpath side, lit at night, that was when it was lit by four lamps at rather long intervals apart. It was jokingly said that they were only lit on moonlight nights. I used to give a sigh of relief when I reached the top after coming off a train. Speaking of trains, they used to have long waits there sometimes as all tickets were punched or collected on them at Polegate. So if anyone reached the third lamp post they could be pretty sure of catching the train alright.

I remember a kind of swing gate there, as it was a public right of way. We finally came out on the road near the front entrance of the present tea gardens, then one could go on through the quaint little village of Wannock to the glen. This was a popular place at all times, with the hills on the opposite side of the road if anyone had the desire for hill climbing. On a Good Friday I have watched crowds of people coming round the bend of the road as the trains unloaded them, for it was always a popular resort of such. Days when primroses, cowslips and sweet violets were to be had for the picking.

Footpaths and tracks

Though perhaps that hardly belongs to Polegate, but there was another grand walk from Wannock to Upper Willingdon all along the foot of the hills and through the cornfields etc. The way the Wannock children used to go to school at Upper Willingdon, in the summer months anyway, winter I suppose had to be a long tramp round the roads. How I know is because my husband was one of said school children and he has told me they often had to carry a big basket of laundry to be mangled and picked up again on their return home.

But to return to the old field footpaths, which they were then I believe a right of way. There was another leading off the road just beyond Park Croft House that used to be. I forget if there were two or three fields to cross, but it brought one out near the British Queen. I think a Free Church now stands at or near the old entrance or finish, if coming from Polegate. I think that was much as it took off so much of the road and the old greens on either side always seemed a resting place for gypsies and tramps. The road often seemed to abound with the latter and I, just after leaving school, was often sent on an errand to the vet's at Wilmington - a journey I did not relish for it was terribly lonely with nothing on the roads whatever beyond an occasional horse and cart or tramps.

Oh what a vast difference to the present day. One could then let their cows feed on the grass verge by the roadside providing someone was with them. I recall that father mostly took that job himself of an evening in summer.

On looking back it must have been after I was 14 that I took on the milk round, but it was then I had a craze to go into service. Mother seemed against it, needing my help at home if more babies arrived. Father said let her go, when she tires of it there is always her home to come back to. I took a place at Wannock as a general maid of all work. Wages were 2/- weekly and we arose at 6.00am. My mistress was very good and taught me quite a lot in the cooking line and soon I could manage evening dinners. My master was a true gentleman and they rarely had visitors. Mother managed to get me some clothes for a start as I had to dress as they desired. Clothes and boots were quite cheap then and soon I acquired my own wardrobe. However I began to chafe at my lack of freedom and I stayed there only four months when I had had enough of being in service. My master arrived a few days later and implored me to go back, but I never wanted to go into service again.

I got married at the age of 24 in 1896, when my husband was working for my father. By the time he earned £1 a week I had four children, on which I could manage quite well. Mother died in November 1899 and five years later father re-married a different type of woman and just five months on he passed away aged 56 through a sudden stroke causing haemorrhage of the brain.

Father's death brought some drastic changes for all of us. It was in September 1904 that we moved to a modest farm at nearby at Sessingham. After a few years my husband turned the wilderness into a lovely garden. The rough access lane in 1923 thereabouts was made into a good hard road and we struggled on for years. It was during the 1914-1918 war the things improved for us as farmers, although our two eldest lads had volunteered for active service and we did not see them for four years until April 1919.

When he died father had amassed a healthy £8,000 and this helped his family considerably. But fortune was not smiling on us when we had to terminate our farming activities. In late March 1957 we had not complied with new rules and regulations concerning the selling of milk - after more than forty years we were banned and we had to find a new way of procuring a living.

Hereafter are further glimpses of old Polegate as remembered by myself, Frank Charles Blackwell, son of the writer of the foregoing pages. Written in the year 1976 - near enough 80 years of my life.

As the first born of the foregoing pages of Louisa Jane Blackwell, a truly wonderful woman and mother, I find it amazing how well I remember old Polegate as she describes it. I suppose the first few years of one's life is a very impressionable period and Polegate certainly had not changed much by the time I was able to sit up and take notice.

I well remember Brook Street when it was only a deep rutted cart track, entirely unmade and ploughed up by the constant passage of noisy tip carts loaded with bricks from the yard at the far end. Actually I suppose those same bricks were being used to cope with Polegate's growing pains and launch the early efforts to produce the future Polegate which have gone on ever since. I think in fact it was during my last couple of years residence there that Brook Street was finally adopted and made up by the Council. I have distinct recollections of the men and boys playing marbles on quite a good surface on traditional Good Friday mornings. There had been however a brick paved sidewalk each side in front of the existing houses. A fact incidentally and indirectly almost resulting in the premature end of my life.

Of the two cottages that mother mentions as being built by grandfather, she, on her marriage, became tenant of the one which still is No 9 where I was born. In favourable weather she would put me in my pram and stand it outside on the pavement. It would seem that the small shop and cottage at the other end, now No 5, was built later than the other pair as an addition, as that would be the only explanation for there to be scaffolding there some two years after No 9 was occupied by my parents - the point being that I apparently owe my existence to a tub of earth often used to plant the wooden scaffold poles in those days. A bolting horse had broken free of its vehicle, but still standing with the broken shafts swinging and banging against its hind quarters. This added to its terror and the horse came charging down Cross Street and unable to negotiate the sharp turn down Brook Street, would certainly have demolished the pram and myself had the tub of earth not absorbed the full impact.

Having escaped that early extinction I started my schooling at the age of three years. As time went on we had pretty much the freedom of Polegate, which with a few others my own age I proceeded to explore and no doubt made a general nuisance of ourselves.

Starting near at home, the gardens of the three cottages ran right down to the stream that gave the street its name. I have cause to remember the stream having at a very tender age pulled my even younger brother out of it, up the steep nettle strewn banking. The stream being at the time at summer level, no real harm was done except us both being badly stung by the nettles and my brother smelling horribly as the ditch in those early and unenlightened days served as the main sewer for the whole of Brook Street. This matter also became unpleasantly apparent after one of the periodical floodings.

Escapades around Brook Street

Beyond the ditch, and between it and the railway, was a strip of market gardens with a number of greenhouses at the far end and beyond that the brickyard. With the railway line in full view from the garden we children would watch in wonder and speculation as to just when the evening mail train would split in two, as surely it did at that time. The front half I believe going straight on, without stopping, to Hastings on the now disused track, the loop line from Hampden Park not existing then. The other half was braked to a standstill at Polegate Station and then taken on to Eastbourne by another engine or possibly coupled with a Hailsham train.

The old sleeper built shed in which grandfather had first housed his cows was still standing, but used as a storage garden shed. The cows having been moved to new quarters at New Barn joined by others as Polegate's need for milk grew. New Barn stood at the bend of Sayerland Road, at the north west corner of what became Sayerlands Estate. I well remember watching cows being milked and watching my father ferreting for rabbits in the fields there. On such occasions should father finally notice that my hands and nose were blue with the cold I was sent back to knock at the door of the Old Thatch where I was soon warmed beside a roaring log fire. Kindly old Mrs Wood produced delicious cakes straight from the oven and she fussed as if I was one of her own brood.

Returning to Brook Street I believe it safe to say that Polegate's milk supply was from the old shed behind No 5 and that my mother was probably the first official milk roundsman. Later No 5 became the first dairy shop with a lad employed delivering milk in pints and half pints from a smart brass churn on a barrow. Sometimes I helped father do this round. I find the old slaughter house and stables still stand down between No 3 and No 5.

As a small child with the occasional half penny or farthing to spend in Mr Tolhurst's bread and confectionery shop or Mr Taylor's grocery on the respective corners of No 5 Cross Street were as two opposing magnets to me. Should I patronise Mr Taylor for value in dried apple rings or locust beans, or should a toffee apple from Tolhurst's or perhaps hundreds and thousands? At the rear of the confectionery shop was the bakery where Mr Caffyn seemed to do everything from crisp loaves to making the many sweets for the shop, to obliging customers baking cakes or roasting their Sunday joints for a few pence.

Across the High Street facing down Brook Street was a timber shed where another Mr Taylor plied his trade as carpenter and next to that was a clump of willows. From the carpenters shed, right round to the Hailsham railway bridge there was only the Polegate Inn, known as The Dinkum, and the blacksmith's forge and cottage. The square of fenced grazing land enclosed by the two roads and railways we always referred to as Davey's field, although it was rented by Mr Tolhurst who allowed village children to use it as a playing area.

Lads at large

We boys found Davey's field a good vantage point to watch the fussy engine shunting full trucks of coal or produce into the goods yard over the fence. Grandfather had the contract to transport coal from there to the new waterworks at Friston and his team took building materials over there when the pumping station was built. Always ensuring of any waste of time with the return wagons loaded with flints from the hill farms to be used by the Council for road making. On the Brook Street side of High Street were half dozen shops although by the time they were completed I only clearly recall Puttocks (or Putmans), that was mainly a chemists, where Barclays is now. Others there were a bookshop, the butchers owned by the Banks family. Mr Tolhurst's walled-in garden filled the remaining square bounded by Cross Street and the road from the High Street emerging as it still does opposite the Polegate Inn. Beyond that was the old corrugated iron Congregational Church and then two or three small shops. At the top corner was a rather grim looking building which I believe (although I am not sure) was first built as a workhouse, but in my time was being used as a laundry by a Mrs Watkins. In fact the junction with the Hailsham Road was then known as Watkin's Corner. Incidentally that road was at that time the only road to Hailsham and beyond. Only much later was the railway bridge and connecting road from Lewes added to what became the A22.

A picture of Polegate

To go back to Watkins Corner, the old cottage facing down the High Street I remember especially as being completely overgrown by a mass of white climbing roses, which in summer was truly a sight to remember. I do not recall if the house was still occupied. Also I remember that to get a pair of shoes repaired we took them to Mr Holter who worked from a timber shed just beyond the row of terraced homes on the right side of Brook Street. Beyond that was only waste land and finally the brickyard.

Until we all eventually left Polegate, when I was about seven years old, I attended Infants School that stood alone between Watkins Corner and Nelson Terrace. On the other side of the road was nothing but fields except for two cottages at the junction of Sayerland Lane, the rose covered cottage and at the railway bridge the new school. Beyond the railway bridge were two or three larger houses before coming to two rows of terraced houses comprising Station Road, with Junction Road running parallel in the rear. The Junction Hotel, so far as I remember, was the last building in that direction.

Returning to the railway crossing and beyond, I too remember those gala days and flower shows in Diplock's field beside the crossing that are now an imposing row of shops and flats. In those days, with the entire absence of other forms of entertainment, these were truly red-letter days with numerous side-shows and athletic events - the highlight being the seemingly impossible task of climbing the greasy pole to claim the leg of mutton prize dangling from the top. Teas were had in the large hay barn and on at least one occasion girl pipers marched back and forth in their colourful kits and sporrans, saucily cocked bonnets and shiny buckled shoes. The field was privately owned so, except for the gracious loaning of it for such occasions as royal jubilees and coronations, could not be used as a public recreation ground. Beyond Diplock's home field came the two or three small shops (St John's Terrace) and a tiny shop. The entrance drive to Southdown House was well hidden from public view by trees and shrubs. Next finally was the original Horse & Groom. The space now occupied by the present Horse & Groom was just a piece of waste ground were flints brought from the hills by my grandfather's wagons and three horse teams were unloaded. The large flints to be whacked and cracked into useful road-making size by a talkative old chap wearing horn goggles to protect his eyes from the inevitable flying splinters. The old timer always had a cheery word and joke with us children.

On the strip of grass the other side of the Lewes to Brighton road, I too, remember the hefty pole that had doubtless been used as a tollgate, but had by then been discarded. That part of the road was popularly known as the turnpike. If we boys had no more important pilgrimage in mind we would watch the daily coach and four swing round the corner and pull up with a flourish in front of the inn. The first warning of its approach was the coach horn fanfare from far up the road and was the signal for the holsters to have the fresh team ready. It took only a few minutes then to exchange the teams and be away again.

Bonfire nights and Black Path

The small shop I remember chiefly as the only one in Polegate where the necessary fireworks could be obtained for Guy Fawkes night, though it was nothing short of amazing the variety of wares on offer at all other times of the year. The fireworks were much in demand as Polegate then boasted a pretty dedicated Bonfire Society. The bonfire procession always started from the Horse & Groom, headed by the landlord's son dressed as a cavalier riding a pony - much to our envy. The bonfire usually being on land later occupied as a council dump (the ESCC yard).

Black Path had remained much as then, except the original wooden fence had been replaced by the iron one. Actually this must have been done at the beginning of the century as my grandfather, as general contractor, bought some of the decayed wood and used it on our farm at Arlington. St John's Road, like Brook Street and Albert Road, was still a mere dirt track, giving access to more market gardens and greenhouses. It emerged into a green lane onto the Willingdon Road and was used as a short cut by us boys on Saturdays and holidays. We would walk over to Hampden Park to enjoy ourselves around the lake.

Excursions and vehicles

Another popular excursion was to Wannock and up the Downs to pick flowers, or watch with envy more fortunate men and boys tobogganing down the ideal slopes of Donkey Hollow. On the way back we would enter the Glen at the Filching end and pass along it's shady path emerging opposite the Tea Gardens. Between there and Polegate I can only remember a pair of houses, one either side of the road. The one at the corner always seemed to be occupied by people interested in the buying and selling of junk. I remember marvelling at the first car to come chugging, and occasionally toppling over, down the High Street headed by a man with a red flag. Also the butchers van, fitted with wooden forms inside for comfort, and of occasional passengers travelling between East Hoathley and Eastbourne. Not to mention the little horse drawn two-wheeled mail cart collecting local mail each evening from the little Post Office beside Banks butchers shop.

One other recollection is that each summer a large contingent of Jewish youngsters descended on Polegate and boarded with families glad of the extra money. I recall their daily pilgrimage to the railway station to draw their ration of white meat and of the animosity with local boys and barracking and occasional fights causing near riot.

We moved to Arlington to scratch a living on a small farm. Mother's fourth child Bert was born about this time and he was taken back to Polegate to become the first christening at the new Non-Conformist church at the top of the High Street, that we had attended when it was a simple corrugated iron building.

Frank Charles Blackwell, writing in 1972 aged 80 years.

POLEGATE PICTURE LEGACY

In perpetuation of the dedication and foresight of the late Harry Hurdle who collected the Polegate scenes that make-up the majority of this section. The publishers trust that Mr Hurdle would approve of this presentation.
Courtesy of his family and East Sussex Record Office.
Thanks also go to Camera Centre, Hailsham, and to my old letterpress colleague Roger Matthews, for their expertise.

Mr Harry Hurdle with his album.

EAST SUSSEX.

Particulars and Conditions of Sale,

OF

A VALUABLE FREEHOLD BUILDING PROPERTY,

KNOWN AS

THE POLEGATE ESTATE

Situate in the Parish of Hailsham, and occupying an important position, adjoining and immediately around Polegate Station, on the Lewes and Hastings Branch of the London, Brighton, and South Coast Railway, about two hours' journey by Rail from London. Polegate being the Junction of the Branch Lines to Eastbourne four miles, and Hailsham three miles distant.

THE POLEGATE ESTATE comprises about

53 ACRES OF VALUABLE LAND,

Forming the remaining and uncovered portion of an Estate in course of development, and already to a great extent built upon.

About 16 ACRES of which are represented by

BUILDING PLOTS

Already set out, with Roads formed and Sewered, and suitable for the erection of Villas or other Dwelling Houses

ABOUT 26 ACRES OF BUILDING LAND,

In ARABLE & PASTURE, not yet set out in Plots, and about

11 ACRES OF VALUABLE

MARKET GARDEN GROUND

Leased, and Property let on Ground Rents.

The whole commending itself specially to BUILDERS and CAPITALISTS, as a remunerative investment, with promise of large prospective increase in value.

And a portion thereof will be Sold by Auction WITHOUT RESERVE, by

MR. GAUSDEN

IN CONJUNCTION WITH

MR. VENESS,

AT DIPLOCK'S ASSEMBLY ROOMS,

EASTBOURNE,

On THURSDAY, the 28th day of JUNE, 1877,

At 2 for 3 o'clock in the Afternoon.

IN 120 LOTS.

Particulars and Conditions of Sale, with Plans, may be obtained of Messrs. PHILLIPS & CHEESMAN, Solicitors, 23, Havelock Road, Hastings; Messrs. CROSS & WELLS, Architects & Surveyors, Havelock Road, Hastings; Mr. GAUSDEN, Auctioneer, 48, Marina, St. Leonards-on-Sea; Mr. VENESS, Auctioneer, 21, Havelock Road, Hastings; at the Junction Hotel, Polegate; at the Place of Sale; or of Mr. POUND, Brook Street, Polegate, who will shew the property.

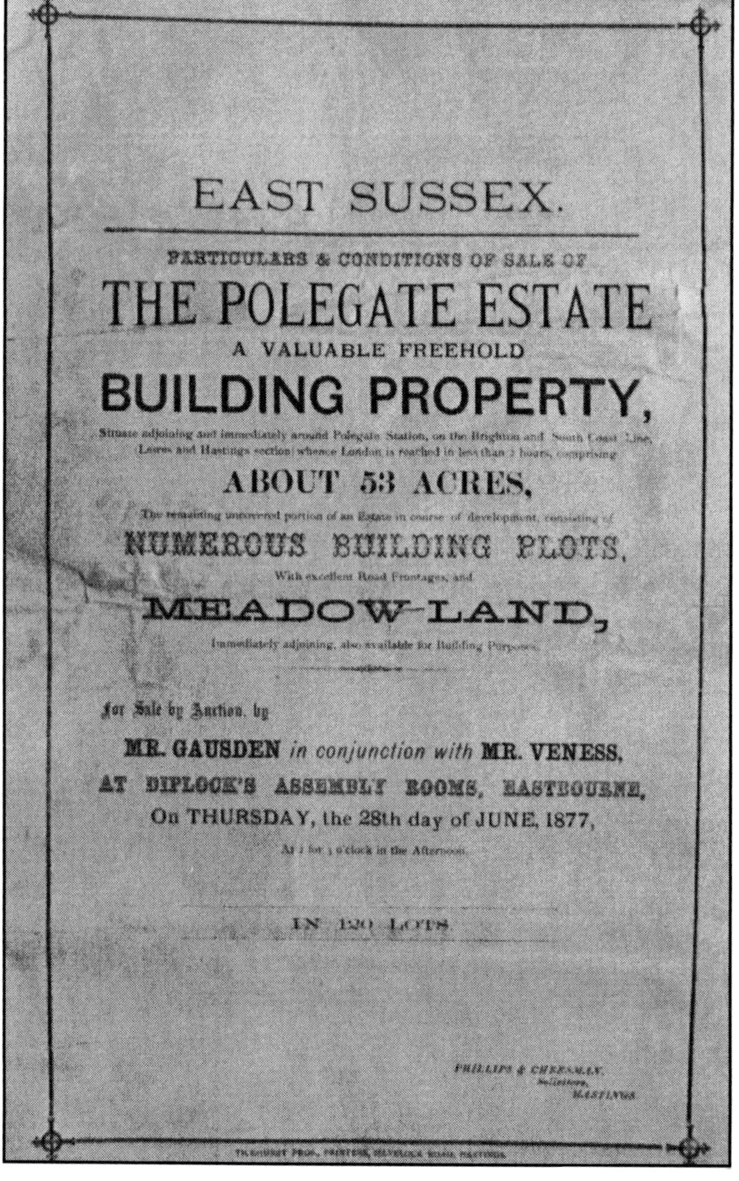

EAST SUSSEX.

PARTICULARS & CONDITIONS OF SALE OF

THE POLEGATE ESTATE

A VALUABLE FREEHOLD

BUILDING PROPERTY,

Situate adjoining and immediately around Polegate Station, on the Brighton and South Coast Line, (Lewes and Hastings section) whence London is reached in less than 2 hours, comprising

ABOUT 53 ACRES,

The remaining uncovered portion of an Estate in course of development, consisting of

NUMEROUS BUILDING PLOTS,

With excellent Road Frontages, and

MEADOW-LAND,

Immediately adjoining, also available for Building Purposes.

For Sale by Auction, by

MR. GAUSDEN *in conjunction with* MR. VENESS,

AT DIPLOCK'S ASSEMBLY ROOMS, EASTBOURNE,

On THURSDAY, the 28th day of JUNE, 1877,

At 2 for 3 o'clock in the Afternoon.

IN 120 LOTS

PHILLIPS & CHEESMAN,
Solicitors,
HASTINGS.

ESRO. AMS 6563/1.

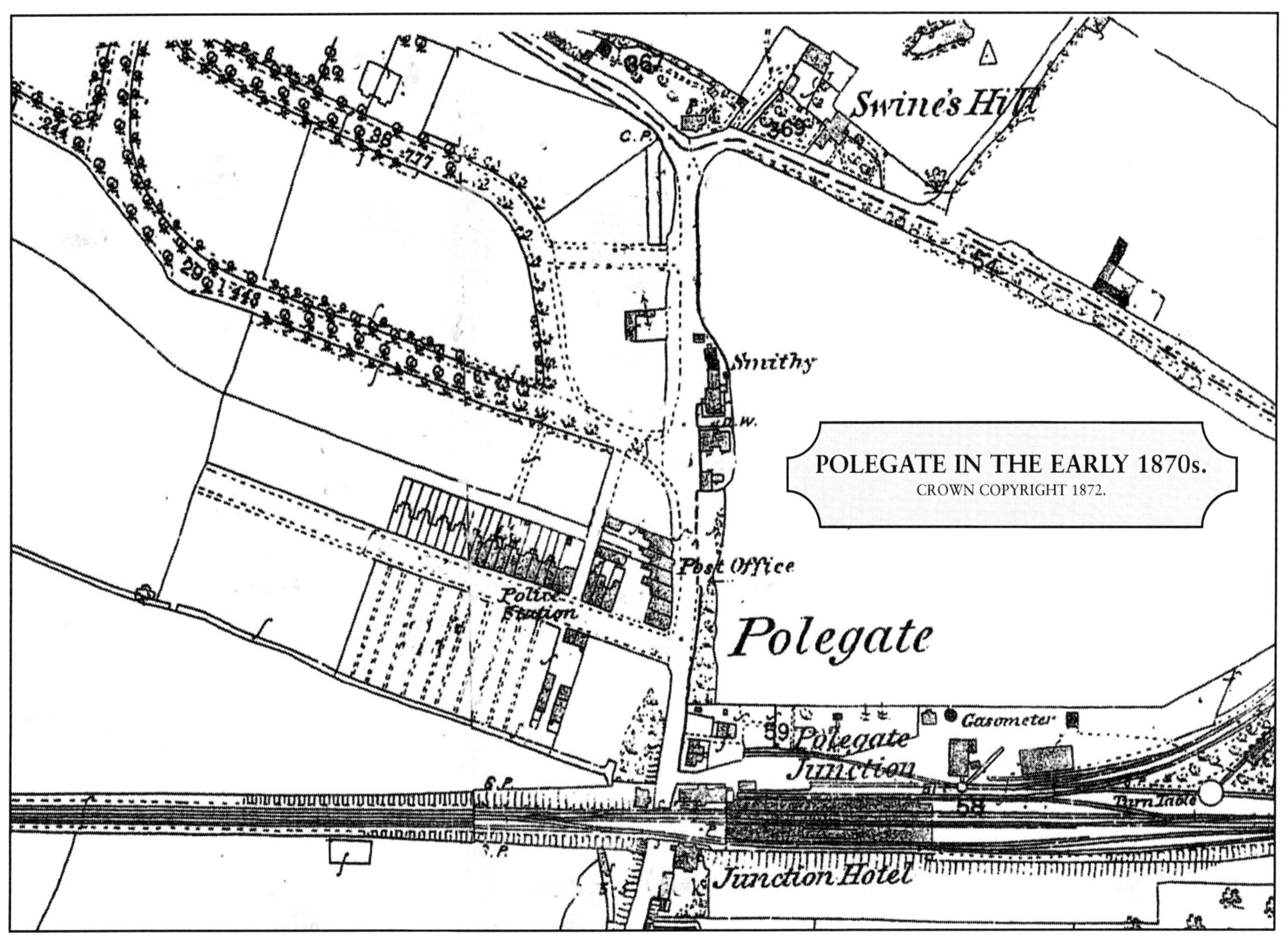

POLEGATE IN THE EARLY 1870s.
CROWN COPYRIGHT 1872.

Top of the High Street, then much as now - and looking up from lower end of the thoroughfare.

The first Horse & Groom went around 1948, but the end of St John's Terrace and St John's Road remains much the same.
ESRO. AMS 6563/1.

More High Street scenes from a century ago - akin to the facing page.

Miss Sarah Diplock's Jubilee Tree is seen facing St John's Terrace.
ESRO. AMS 6563/1.

When tracing buildings their facia may have changed, but roof features are usually recognisable.

Looking down a tranquil Station Road and facing west from the Junction Inn and Junction Stores.

Brickyards were once a familiar aspect of the growing community, this is Gurr's site now occupied by Brookside bungalows.
ESRO. AMS 6563/1.

The junction of Victoria Road and Hailsham Road at Nelson Terrace remains hardly altered.

Whereas going south over the crossing is barely recognisable now.

Waghorn's Garage is depicted in the late 1930s beside the new Horse & Groom.
ESRO. AMS 6563/1.

A tree lined Albert Road in the late 19th century, some of those front walls remain extant.

William Wood's High Street forge and stabling workshops survived to the early 1960s as Capt Handford's taxi premises.

Gradually estate land was acquired for housing development.
ESRO. AMS 6563/1.

A VALUABLE FREEHOLD
BUILDING PROPERTY,
KNOWN AS
THE POLEGATE ESTATE

Situate in the Parish of Hailsham, and occupying an important position, adjoining and immediately around Polegate Station, on the Lewes and Hastings Branch of the London, Brighton, and South Coast Railway, about two hours' journey by Rail from London. Polegate being the Junction of the Branch Lines to Eastbourne four miles, and Hailsham three miles distant.

THE POLEGATE ESTATE comprises about

53 ACRES OF VALUABLE LAND

Structural features of bustling Polegate Junction dominated the community for decades.

The granary store was eventually burnt out in the early 1960s - also surplus were the distinctive station sidings lamp house and the lofty signalling system.

ESRO. AMS 6563/1.

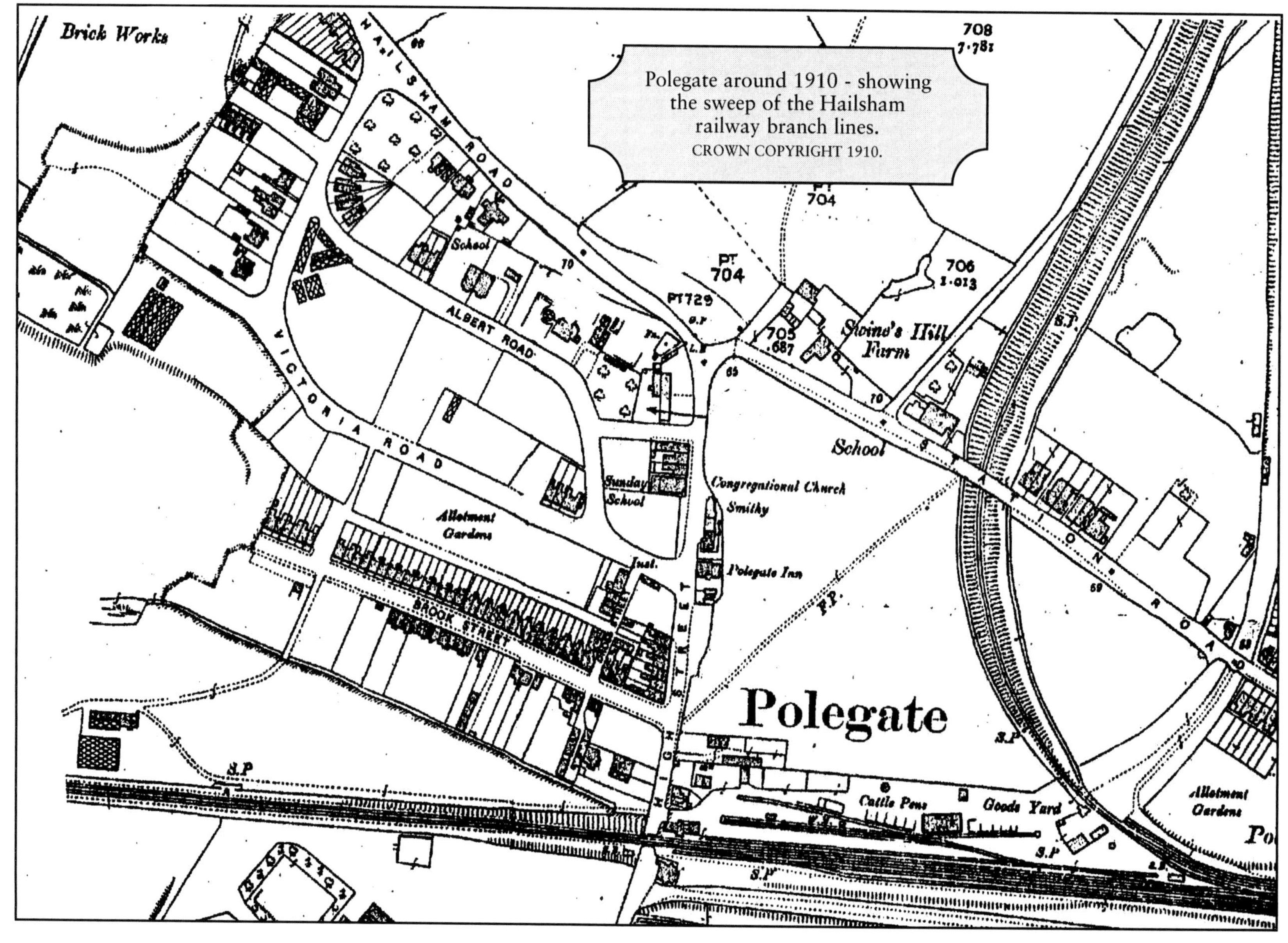

Polegate around 1910 - showing the sweep of the Hailsham railway branch lines.
CROWN COPYRIGHT 1910.

The distant days of crossing gates are recalled in these scenes. Railway workers homes backed onto the line, the simple station platform (similar to Berwick) has already gone in this view, leaving a void.

The single-storey booking office is seen adjacent to the High Street.
ESRO. AMS 6563/1.

A 1928 scene down the High Street - with the Polegate Inn (Dinkum) off centre.
ESRO. AMS 6563/1.

The Cottage in the High Street is seen just before demolition, it may have been an old beer house prior to its next door Railway Arms hostelry. Unfortunately that poignant panel above the porch reveals nothing when computer enhanced.
ESRO. AMS 6563/1.

The familiar sight of Ridley's garage, now AutoWise, developed from Waghorn's Garage built on the plot of the first Horse & Groom seen below.
ESRO. AMS 6563/1.

Southdown Hall, facing the gardens. 1873-1936.
What might Caleb Diplock junior be saying?
ESRO. AMS 6563/1.

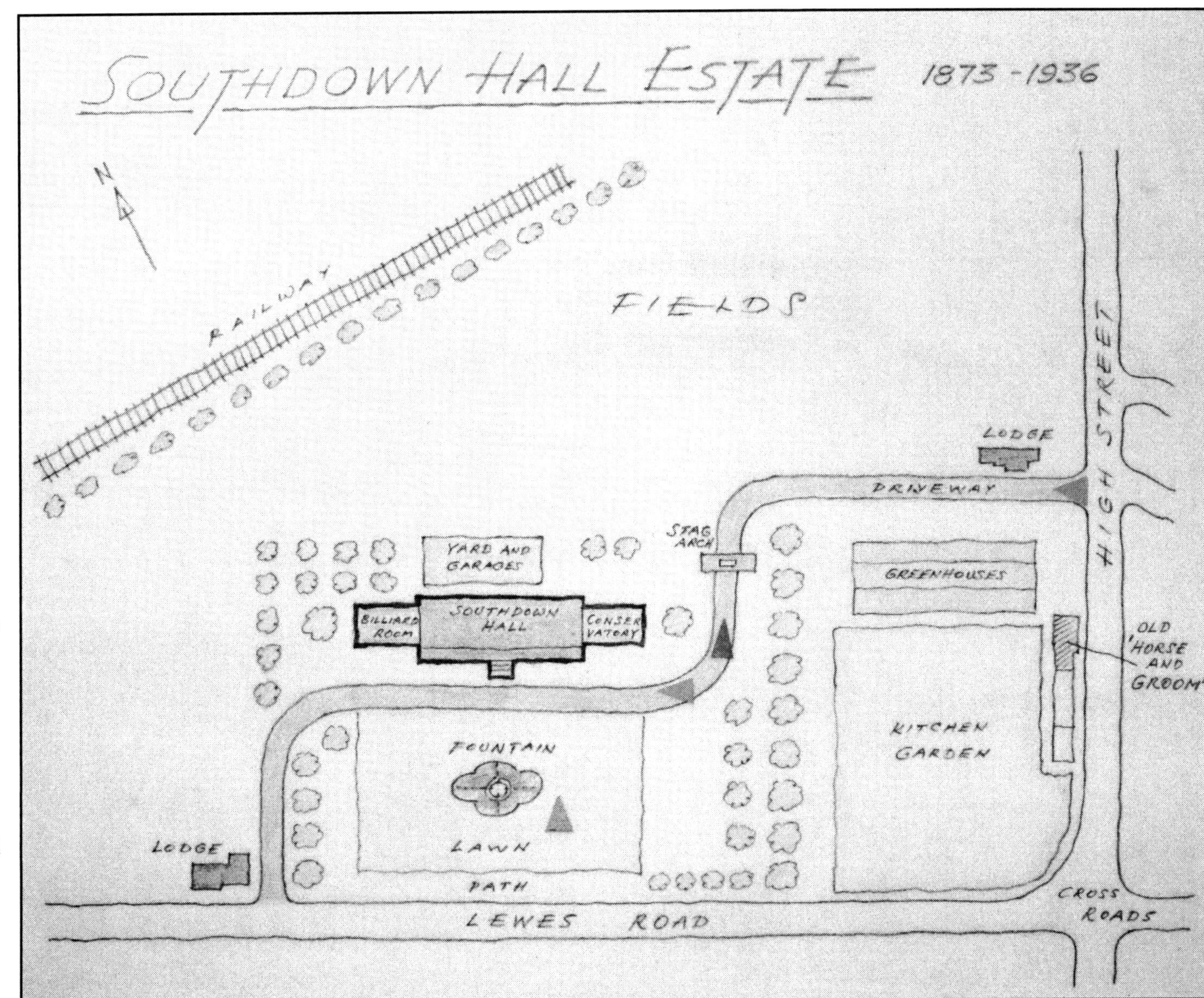

Sadly only the pair of lodge houses remain in situ from the once grandiose Diplock estate.

The Stag over the driveway is extant as a centre piece to the Bernhard Baron Cottage Homes

ESRO. AMS 6563/1.

The first Junction Inn at the end of Black Path (above) was demolished around 1970 when the new shopping precinct was built.
Mrs D. EARL.

Other redundant railway property, now long since removed, cluttered the crossing gates.
ESRO. AMS 656.

The life and times of the second railway station built in the early 1880s. At least the exterior has remained virtually intact.
ESRO. AMS 656.

Wannock watermill is recalled in these scenes prior to its demolition from 1960 for housing as Mill Race, Croft Close, Farmlands Way, Mill Lane, Old Mill Road, Mill Stream Gardens and Park Croft.

Albert Ovenden, the last miller, died in June 1973.
ESRO. AMS 6563/1.

Polegate windmill was undergoing restoration as Operation Weathershield at the time of this compilation.
POLEGATE LIBRARY.

As Park Croft Mill it was captured against the South Downs by Edwin Byatt.
THE MEDICI SOCIETY.

The old Toll House seen at the top of the High Street lasted until 1910, in the 1930s homes were erected close to the site. Swine's Farm House is seen with a 1794 plan by Jonathan Harmer, lower right is School Lane to the current school.
ESRO. AMS 6563/1.

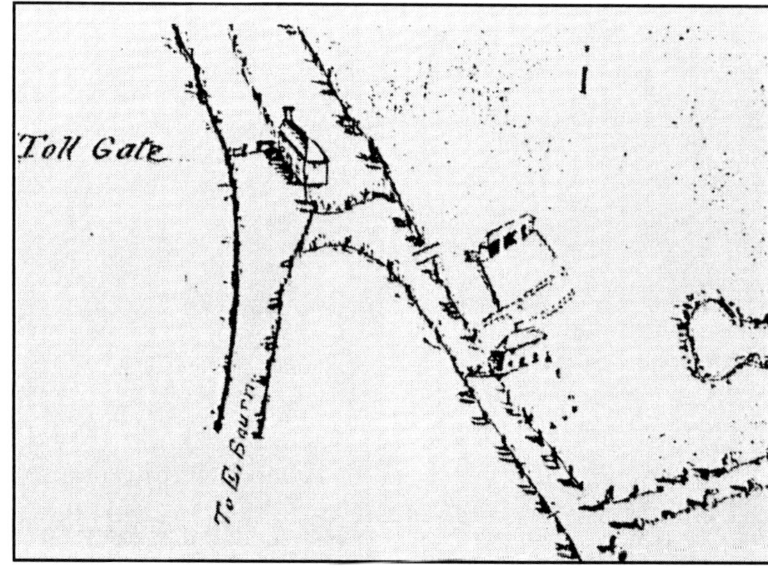

No 11 Brook Street, seen in the mid 1930s, was a popular fishmongers shop. The property has since been demolished.

Woodside Cottages, No 1 and Bedlam, viewed down London Road around that time.

Sayerland House slumbers in private ownership.

Road surfaces were very rough and horse drawn wagons were widely used.
ESRO. AMS 6563/1.

Ernest Randall commenced his carrier business circa 1920 with his de-mob gratuity. He became a popular figure around the village until 1960 when he passed away aged 68 years.
ESRO. AMS 6563/1.

Enterprising Henry Twine built-up a robust local bus service from the mid 1920s.

Gradually though Southdown Co brought out their smaller competitors. Ironically the role was reversed in the mid 1980s.

Henry Twine became a highly successful property developer in Polegate.
ESRO. AMS 6563/1.

Henry Twine, far left, lines up for the camera with some of his bus crew.
ESRO. AMS 6563/1.

The nightmare junction of the A27/A22 that caused many bottlenecks.
Mrs PENNY BARNES.

AA patrol man Arthur Lee was a familiar figure at the Polegate crossroads until traffic lights arrived in late 1964.
ESRO. AMS 6563/1.

Trading terminated from Polegate Motors in mid September 1987 to clear the site for a new Esso store and petrol station facility. Brian Petch, managing director of Polegate Motors, became licensee of the new garage.

The firm had been on the same site since 1946 when Eric Petch, his father, started in business - eventually selling the freehold to Esso.
HAILSHAM GAZETTE.

The present Tesco Express & Esso Service Station opened July 9th 2001. Bringing the consumer-led concept of modern day retailing access to the community.
GOTEHOUSE.

In 1922 numbers 10 and 12 High Street, seen above, had an addition built to the left as No 14 beside Black Path. On this plot is currently the Sloane's Square store. In the mid 1980s as Buckley's News the basement area spawned the novel and resourceful Museum of Shops that moved on to larger premises with greater potential at Battle in East Sussex.
ESRO. AMS 6563/1.

No 12 High Street (below) was run by members of Fred Hill's family for almost eighty years.
Mrs ANNETTE BUCKLEY.

Osborne House, in Albert Road, was built in 1869 for Mr William Attwood in elegant Italianate style modelled on Queen Victoria's Isle of Wight retreat. The property became a dinosaur to maintain and was demolished around 1961 to make way for the Osborne Court flats.

ESRO. AMS 6563/1 and POLEGATE LIBRARY.

A chalet, appropriately named Winsome (below) and small holding, was created in Albert Road in the mid 1920s. It had been a prize in a Tit-Bits magazine Targets contest won by a Mr Hall. In 1987 the site was cleared and built over as Chiltern Court flats.

ESRO. AMS 6563/1.

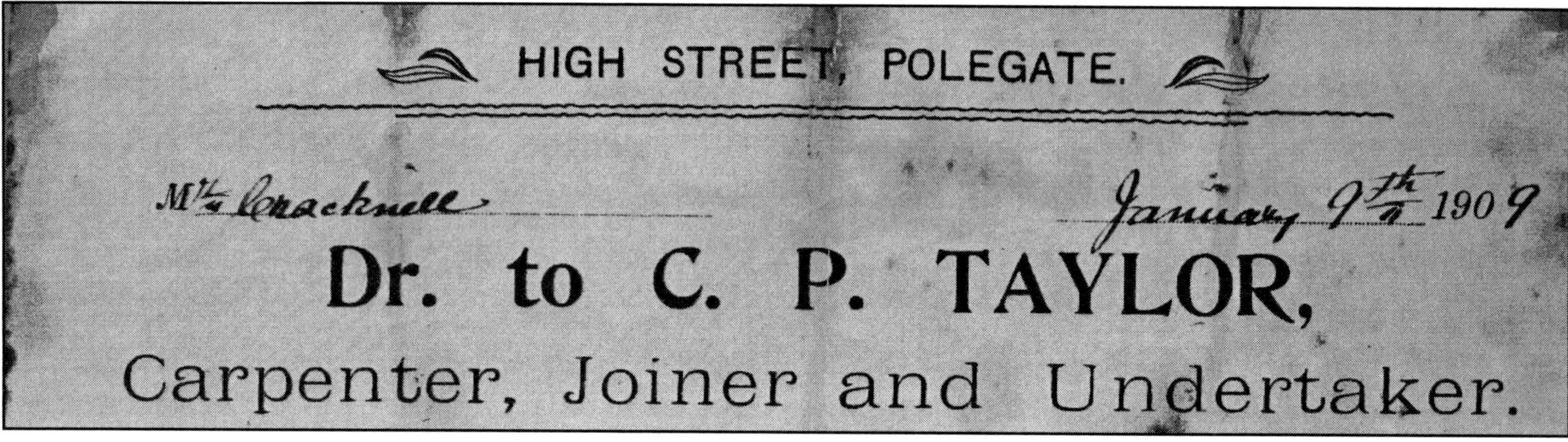
HIGH STREET, POLEGATE.

Mrs Cracknell January 9th 1909

Dr. to C. P. TAYLOR,

Carpenter, Joiner and Undertaker.

The Taylor and Wood families were amongst the most prolific locally. Cornelius Taylor lived at 59 High Street and was the popular leader of many local activities. The building itself has had numerous uses over the years. The site has been known as Watkin's Corner.

ESRO. AMS 6563/1.

Artisans terraced residences in Brook Street that was one of the first roads laid out in the 1870s and lead to Gurr's brick works.

Rendering conceals many secrets from the past - No 4 on the corner with Cross Street once bustled as Taylor's hardware store for some eighty years.
ESRO. AMS 6563/1.

The loss of the old school buildings in the early 1990s was controversial. That foundation stone above can be seen on the buildings that replaced it in School Lane. The single storey hut, left, was the school hall.
ESRO. AMS 6563/1 & Mrs WENDY SMITH.

The younger people of Polegate have always played a vital role in the village - and then the town. Maybe today their expectations are beyond our resources . . .
ESRO. AMS 6563/1.

Rustic Polegate once featured numerous plant nurseries and laundries serving large houses and Eastbourne hotels.

Queensmead has been built on a nursery plot and St Leonards Laundry once serviced the area.
ESRO. AMS 6563/1.

The changing pace of Polegate High Street - sixty years separate these scenes. 1900-1960.

Mrs PENNY BARNES.

&

ESRO. AMS 6563/1.

Looking west towards the South Downs in the late 1930s reveals so many features of interest.
ESRO. AMS 6563/1.

C.F. Taylor, Gentlemen's Hairdresser,
was a memorable High Street
feature for over
fifteen years.
The property facia numeration
relates to its Gilda Parade
position.
Mrs ANNETTE BUCKLEY.

Is this the way to the fabled Treacle Mines?
Land around Polly Arch was a childrens' haunt for many innocent adventures.
More recently it has attracted interest from the auctioneer's hammer.

The first Polegate School has been saved and is currently used as a place of worship.
GOTEHOUSE.

Cross Street particularly has an interesting heritage, notably No 4 seen here retains its original format.

Poor old Red Croft in St John's Road has passed its century and is now being re-developed. Imagine the aura off that balcony towards the Downs in its heyday. Demolition took place in late September 2004.

Mrs MAUREEN COPPING.

Polegate is well-served with pubs and clubs and they tend to go through phases of popularity. The second oldest must be The Junction, whilst the Horse & Groom is perhaps busiest now. The more recent Thoroughbred is the most difficult to photograph agreeably.

GOTEHOUSE.

It may be hard to visualise but The Dinkum retained its 1847 Railway Arms frontage until Harvey's Brewery undertook a frontal makeover in 1979 and adopted the local sobriquet as The Dinkum.
Mrs MAUREEN COPPING

St John's Parish Church, together with St George's Catholic Church and United Reformed Church, accommodate the towns spiritual and many social needs.
GOTEHOUSE

The town sign, designed by Ron Randall, was first installed on a verge outside St George's Church, but has now been re-sited opposite The Horse & Groom.

In mid 1999 an 800 strong petition fought to to save the Wheatley Elm in St John's Road. Town councillors faced the dilemma of a £85 fee to fell the tree, but opted for the £45 charge to prune the growth. Ironically that October a deadly honey fungus was discovered on the tree and it was felled by ESCC contractors.
VERA HODSOLL.

ROYAL NAVAL AIR SERVICE - POLEGATE

In 1915 the British Government needed suitable sites for airship stations to protect Allied shipping. A 142 acre plot just south of Polegate was selected for its downland shelter and road and rail links. Work started during 1915 and dominated WWI activity around the village. Men and women were billeted in the community and their uniforms, supplies, duties, transit and social life played their part locally.

The most notable incident involved a tragic mis-judgement amid foggy conditions on December 20th 1917 when two airships collided . The old transport repair workshop in Coppice Avenue survived as Bird Engineering Co premises into the mid 1990s and only a few artefacts, like odd mooring posts, remain from that gallant era. There are several worthy accounts from that time by RNAS Polegate personnel on local library shelves.

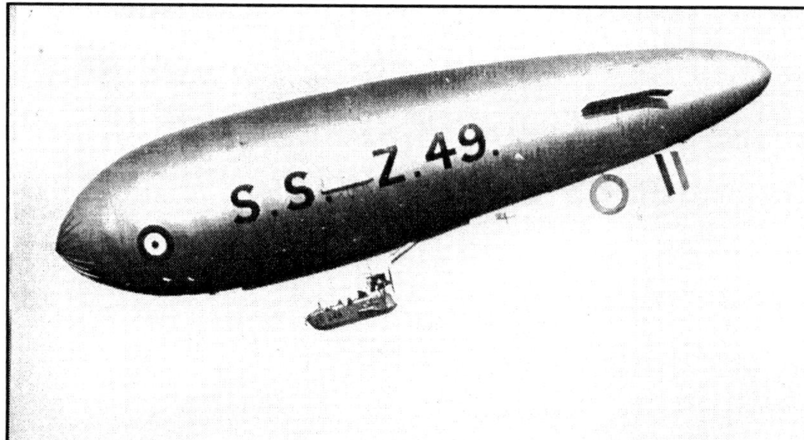

A mooring post relic of RNAS Polegate unearthed recently on the Donkey Hollow escarpment.

A delicate landing - note that gondola.

The former transport repair workshop survived as Bird Engineering Co until the mid 1990s, now Scanlon Close occupies the site.

Via RON BISHOP.

An airmen's view of RNAS Polegate at Lower Willingdon - the former A22 can be seen top right.
Via RON BISHOP.

Probably the worst incident in Polegate during WWII occurred on January 23rd 1943. Four low flying Focke Wulf 190s aircraft made their mark on 17-19 Western Avenue on Southlands Estate and wrecked a pair of recently built semi-detached bungalows. The attack was intended for Hailsham four miles north, but due to a navigational error Polegate became the fatal target. Amongst the casualties was a Gunner Stanley Gifford of the Royal Canadian Artillery who had married a local lady just six months earlier. Two local civilians that died were Margaret Bridger and Caroline Thorpe. One of the escaping enemy aircraft was brought down by light AA fire off Beachy Head and its pilot was killed when they crashed into the sea.

Allied aircraft incidents around the village were numerous and many, many, fighters landed around the fields. Beachy Head was a natural landmark for airmen. Eastbourne district became a fatal target for enemy pilots and the communities suffered heavily. On February 2nd 1944 a returning USAAF Liberator B-24 bomber was attempting to land at RAF Friston, but struck the top of the Downs near Butts Brow. Ten young American airmen were killed and two died later of their injuries.

On August 31st 1943 groups of USAAF B-17s were assembling over Beachy Head. One collided with another bomber and turned inland, coming down on farm land at Wootton Manor where it struck anti invasion poles and woodland. All eight airmen died in that incident.

On February 6th 1945 an outward bound RAF Douglas Dakota, KG630, struck downland in fog and careered to the foot of the escarpment at Middle Brow, Folkington. All twenty-three young airmen died in the inferno.

By coincidence on May 6th 1945 another Dakota struck the top of the hills, above the Long Man outline, and claimed four USAAF airmen.

Many local people still have vivid memories of WWII. Of Allied troops from all outposts of the globe billeted or in transit around Polegate.

The mixture of brogues and languages, Of the numerous district large houses that were requisitioned, of camps, bombing and aircraft incidents, rationing - plus ARP activities centred around the old Horse & Groom.

Perhaps one of the least acknowledged roles during those years of hardship, and conflict was the industrious Women's Land Army, seen here gathered formally and at Gosford Nurseries.
Via TONY BONIFACE.

Local scenes involving aspects of team work - are any faces recognisable?

Polegate Auxiliary Fire Service had their station alongside the present doctors' surgery, whilst the football players remain from an unknown side.
Via TONY BONIFACE

In October 2000 the Town Council moved into their new offices in the High Street and gradually the facilities there have been developed.

The Centre shopping block opened in 1969 and the precinct is like a town meeting venue for news and lively gossip . . .

It was back in 1975 that the Polegate Community Centre extension was opened.

GOTEHOUSE.

Polegate Post Office has been empty since March 2003 and people wonder who will move into the premises. It was built with 30 foot deep foundations to take a first floor, but we do not need any such intrusion.

Much of the text for this account came from Polegate Library. In March 2001 the library re-opened after a major refit.
POLEGATE LIBRARY.

Seen at the 1986 opening of the library are Bill Daly, Miss Hardingham, Vera Hodsoll, Branch Librarian, Mr Russell, the County Librarian and seated Parish Councillors Mr & Mrs L. Moore.
POLEGATE LIBRARY.

Polegate Junction has moved on from railways to highways. Cophall area has become the future? Planning applications for development there have been lodged for many years. The £17.3m bypass, opened in mid 2002, to carry 20,000 vehicles daily that once choked the town.

Curious stockade like hoardings appeared on approach roads early in 2004. Was Polegate becoming a cowboy town - or was it to protect those Treacle Mines?

GOTEHOUSE.

To close this archive a scene from almost a century ago - diverse Polegate people of all generations.

So is this the way to the Treacle Mines? Many passers-by must be curious about the igloo like ESCC store for road salt compound.
GOTEHOUSE.

URBAN ARCHIVE - POLEGATE

Dates expressed herein are known periods of occupancy derived from local directories, news reports, church magazines and personal interviews.

Our thanks are conveyed to business people who responded to a Questionnaire*.

Property numbers can change over a period of time - e.g. Station Road(s), Gilda Parade (High Street).

High Street numeration altered between publication of Kelly's Directories of 1955-1957 and 1972-1973.

Compiled by Peter Longstaff-Tyrrell with Maureen Copping. E. & O.E.

The retail revolution - additions and updates are invited . . .

POLEGATE MISCELLANY

Properties old and new around the town at the time of the first printing, indicating recent changes in the High Street and on former railway land for residential uses.

HIGH STREET - ODD NUMBERS

To locate . . .
WILLIAM LAURENCE, grocer, 1946.
W. MILLAR, confectioner, 1932.
A.J. PAYNE, builders, 1937.
SOUTHDOWN CARAVAN & TRAILER CO, High Street, 1937.
SWORDER & DAVIS, tea rooms, 1935-1937.
WISSAM, bootmakers, High Street, 1937.

1. HORSE & GROOM public house. 1935-2004. Licensee Mrs K. Hemmings 1937. Erected on open fields beside crossroads, circa 1935 when the road was widened and titled A22 Polegate bypass, which took through traffic out of the village. The hostelry was built to the design of the brewery architect Herbert Crompton. To emphasise the name he incorporated a couple of stucco panels in the south elevation showing in each a horse and groom. An undated horse trough extant outside the premises states Metropolitan Drinking Fountain and Cattle Trough Association, is currently utilised as a flower display by the local branch of the Women's Institute.

3. AUTOWISE motor vehicle servicing, 1994-2004. Previously C.L. RIDLEY & SON, Volvo car agents. 1980-1997. Previously Waghorn's garage and Service Station, proprietors A.J. & P.J. Wright 1973. Motor cycle specialist, proprietor E.H. Waghorn, 1921-1973. Occupying the site of the original Horse & Groom Inn, built in 1819, demolished 1948. Licensees: George Fowler, 1899; Charles Smith, 1887-1893; Thomas Vine, 1887; Alexander Hurst, 1882; William Humphrey, 1866; William Bodle, 1850-1858; Benjamin Tutt, 1839;

5. MORGAN VINE, butcher, 1924-1955. J.F. BANKS, butcher, 1918.

Old Drive, flats and bungalows, also site of former telephone exchange.

7. POLEGATE PHOTOGRAPHIC & VIDEO*. Proprietors Roger White and Jon Murrell, August 2001-2004. Briefly dog parlour CANINE CAPERS, beauticians for pets, proprietors Annette Gerry and Judith Vincent, 2001. BYGONES, second-hand house furniture, proprietor Tony (Arthur) Moore, 1981-2000. LAURENCE BARTON, butcher, 1937-1955. Mr Hunt, butcher, 1937. W.H. CAREY & SON, butcher, 1927. HENRY COLBRAN, butcher, 1924.

9. F. WINGROVE, baby's and ladies garments, 1967-2004, proprietor Fred Wingrove. Also known as No 4 St John's Terrace, built circa 1875 by Mr Wingrove's grandparents, trading as Yetton and also Mrs E.M. WARREN, general shop, 1935-1937, PERCIVAL WARREN, general shop, 1946. No 4 was demolished and rebuilt in 1951 as 9 High Street.

11-13. Private homes, St John's Terrace and St John's Cottages.
County Police, P.C. J. Mayne 1918. Charles Gold, boot maker, 1899. Elizabeth Yetton, dealer of toys, 1899.

15. HOUSE & MORTGAGE CENTRE and TOWN & COUNTRY Estate Agents. 2004. WYATT & SONS, estate agents, 1994. L.M. FARNHAM, estate agents and auctioneers, 1967-1973. The larger corner premises are recalled as being Alliance & Leicester estate agents 1994. MEYERS, estate agents, 1981-1995.

15a. For many years the smaller shop was STREBOR Gentlemen's Hairdresser, proprietor Fred Roberts, 1965-1988. Mr Roberts was forced out of his premises by estate agents who, it is said, wanted the unit themselves.

Two blocks of neighbouring flats known as Elizabeth Court, eight flats in all. Built by Henry Twine in the 1960s and named after his daughter-in-law Elizabeth who had married his son Rex. The site of Caleb Diplock's Home Field.

Block of ten maisonettes with retail outlets below completed in 1963:-
29. STRINGTOWN SUPPLIES*, outdoor clothing, camping kit, army surplus goods etc. 1994-2004, takes its name from the rope making town of Hailsham where they started business, proprietor Clive Hodson. Previously the shop was FRANKIS ladies footwear shoemakers, 1965-1983, proprietor Mrs Audrey Frankis.

31. POLEGATE FISHERIES, take-away fish and chips, also eat-in facilities, 1981-2004. BROADWAY FISHERIES, fishmongers, 1967-1973.

33. WITHERS D.I.Y., ironmongers, 1980-2004. Jack and Ernie, 1986. Proprietors Jill and Jack Collier, 1983. Previously HYSON HARDWARE 1972-1980. LESTER D-I-Y, 1972-1973. PRICE BARGAIN STORE 1968, proprietor J.F. Cassidy. F.A. PRICE, hardware, 1967.

35-37. ONE-STOP CONVENIENCE STORES, 2001-2004. Tim Smith trading as Londis ran this shop from about 1994 to 2001, after moving over from No 10 opposite. Previously KITCHEN, BATHROOM & HEATING CENTRE, NU GAS central heating, plumbing, proprietors Michael and Peter O'Driscoll, 1980-1986. W.J. BRACEY & SON, grocers, 1967-1973. G.L. PAGE, V.G. Grocers, 1970. HUDSON'S FOODS, grocers, 1963-1965.

39. HAIRLINES, ladies and gents hairdressing. Formerly Hairlines & Alexander, 1972. GABRIEL, ladies hairdresser, 1967-1973.

41. LLOYDS TSB Bank, 1967-2004. ALFRED SAYERS, fishmonger, 1959.

45. LADBROKES Betting shop, 2004. Formerly POLEGATE RACING. B. STOCK OFF-COURSE, turf accountant, 1973. J. CLARK, turf accountants, 1967.

47. CARDS, GIFTS BOOKS. J.H.P. Cards and Books, proprietor Heath Pye, 1987-2004. GATEWAY CLEANERS, proprietors G.R and J.G. Stock, 1968-1973. VALERIE, lingerie, 1967.

Railway signal box and crossing. Signal box built in 1883 styled by Saxby and Farmer, unusual design having pointed arches to locking windows.

Allotments.

49. POLEGATE TOWN HALL, 1999-2004. Purchased for the controversial sum of £120,000.
At rear B.M. HEPBURN Ltd plastering contractors, 1998-2004. Previously 49-51, STONEWALL GARDEN CENTRE, 1993-1999.
also 49-57. GEORGE GATES & SONS, building materials, 1957-1977. GEORGE GATES, joiner, 1937.

53. BEEJAY CARPETS, 1981, occupied part of the site before Harte Read extended their premises circa 1984. POLEGATE HEALTH FOOD STORES, 1973. M.S. BARNETT, physician and surgeon, 1967. PHILIP HUBBARD, physician and surgery, 1965-1967. HAROLD SHAW, physician and surgery, 1965-1967.

55. HARTE READ & CO. solicitors, 1965-2004. GEORGE HOWARD & CO. estate agents, 1955-1968. BRACKETTS, surveyors, 1973.

57. HSBC, bank, 2002-2004. MIDLAND BANK, 1965-2002.

Brook Street.

59-61. BARCLAYS BANK, 1924-2004. They took over the second unit (No 61) to make the current site. One unit was a grocers prior to Barclays taking over. Circa 1905, WALKERS GROCERS. Circa 1880s recalled as either PUTTOCKS (or Putmans) that was mainly a chemist. This block it thought to have been built around 1860 after the railway developed and is shown on the Ordnance Survey map of 1872.

61. R.F. BLACKISTON, estate agents, auctioneers, 1965-1967. G.B. (Eastbourne), estate developers, 1965. POLEGATE PLANT HIRE, 1967. Bank was later extended to occupy No 61. Circa 1880s a book shop.

61a. SAXON-GIBBS, builders, 1967. GARDENCRAFT, gardeners, 1965-1967.

63. SUMMER'S ANTIQUES, Richard Millis, October 2004. DEVOTEDLY DISCUS & POLEGATE PETS, proprietor Sadde Truss, in September 2004 this business moved across the road to the former Fairways premises. POLEGATE PETS, 1995. Polegate Pet & Garden centre, proprietors Keith Pyle and Eric Wall, 1970-1980. Formerly HAILSHAM RADIO, proprietors D. and M. Dean, 1959-1973.

63a. H.S. APPLIN, building contractors, 1967. E.J. PHAROAH, plant hire, 1967.

65. EXPRESS CLEANERS & SHOE REPAIRS, dry cleaners, 1997-2004. BRACKETTS, estate agents, 1973. Formerly F.C. TAYNTON & SONS, shoe repairs 1963-1977. R.J. BLAND & SON, shoe care and repair, established 1939. 1959-67.

67. SMITHERS butchers, 2003-2004. Briefly butchers run by Adrian Steel. Previously MORGAN VINE 1935-2003, family butchers.

69. PROCTORS, chemist, 1973-2004. Previously ARTHUR MILLS chemist, 1959-1970. REGINALD BECK, chiropodist, 1959. EVERARD VENN CLAYDON, physician and and surgery, 1965.

71. SLOANE'S SQUARE*, Internet cafe and delicatessen, proprietor Ms Sloane Bridle, 2003-2004. Briefly SEABREEZE FISHERIES, wet fish shop, 2002-2003. Previously PARAPHERNALIA, domestic and fancy goods, 2001. STILL'S, electrical supplies and service, 1993. TV & ELECTRICAL CENTRE, 1986. TV & ELECTRICITY CENTRE, partners D. Christie and J.M. Wells, October 1983. BEX ELECTRICAL CENTRE/M.E. COLEMAN, 1963-1981.

This block of retail units and flats was completed by Bill Applin in 1959. Mr Hanning-Beck, a chemist, had brought the plot of land - a former orchard - for £1,000. The whole block cost £11,000 to build.

71a. D.B. DOMESTICS, household electrical equipment, 2002-2004. Previously ART & GLASS SHOP, proprietor Elaine Hanaghan, 1998-1999. POLEGATE PANTRY, proprietors Mike and Pauline Reed 1986-1987. Previously as POLEGATE PANTRY, proprietor Audrey Chant 1986. DAVIDSON'S 1984-1986. Pauline and Stewart Keates, 1974-. V.G. GROCERS, Proprietors G.F. and R.C. Fisher, 1972. Mrs & Mrs B.H. DAVID took over the business of Mr Page in 1971. G.L. PAGE, Grocers, 1960-1971.

73. L. & M.T. STRETTON, newsagents and stationery, 1999-2004. Sheila and Bob to about 1993, then sold to Stretton's. Formerly R.&.S.TAGG newsagents, proprietors Sheila and Robert Tagg, 1981-1983. WALTER GIBBONS, newsagents, 1959-1979.

On this corner was formerly Marshall's Nursery. Bill Applin built the modern block of flats and shops in 1958. Some frontage is in Victoria Road, although the address is High Street.

73a. MAGPIES, second hand furniture, 2003-2004. Previously BROOKS CARPETS, 2003. SEABREEZE FISHERIES, proprietor David Dobbs, wet fish shop, 2001. SWAG SHOP, proprietor Monica Crumpling. 50p SHOP. closed February 1999. In early 1999 the shop owner, Gordon Worcester, had offered to make the premises into a Youth Cafe for the community. However agreement with the town council could not be achieved in time. Unknown name - domestic upholstery/fabrics store, 1995? KNIGHTS wallpaper and paints specialists, proprietor Mrs Maureen Rhodes, 1981-1986. Previously K. WALTON, domestic decorating supplies, 1959-1977, Keith Walton being the original occupier of the premises.

75. GLENISTER'S, florist, 1997-2004. Previously TAYLORS, fruiterer and greengrocers, proprietors Harold and Howard Taylor (father and son), 1967-1983. Run by the son and mother until about 1989. Then taken over by Bruce and Rene Pullen as greengrocers and florist until about 1989.

77. DOWNLANDS MEDICAL CENTRE. Doctors Surgery. 2004. Previously building was occupied by BRIGHTON EQUITABLE CO-OPERATIVE SOCIETY, 1938-1977 - re-opened at The Centre 22nd May 1977. Situated between what is now the Downland Medical Centre and the United Reformed Church was the shed like premises of the WWII National Fire Service station that would exit from Albert Road when required.

Flats above named Malcolm Court.

Malcolm Court was built in 1966 by Malcolm Pearce builders.

79. DAVID P. BUCK*, gentlemen's wear, proprietors Mr & Mrs David P. Buck 1971-2004. Previously BERNARD SHADWELL men's wear, 1960-1971. THEAKER, chemist, 1967.

81. POLEGATE OFF-LICENCE, proprietor K.S. Davies, 2003-2004. Previously RICHARD'S WINE STORE and before that for many years UNWINS off-licence 1971-1973.

83. SIMPLY BEAUTY 2004, beauty parlour, previously JOVONNE'S hairdressers, 2003. TONER'S his and hers hair specialists, 1981. AMANDA JANE, ladies hairdresser, 1973. Formerly PARSONS, ladies hairdressers, 1965-1970.

85. JOVONNES hairdressers, 2004. Previously BRADLEY HONE, estate agents, 1998-2003. M.E. COLEMAN, Television Service Centre, 1983. LYNLEYS, jewellers, 1965. KERN, jewellers, 1973. N.G. POOLE, Lynleys jewellers, 1962-1967.

United Reformed Church, previously Congregational Church between 1904-1981.

87. SINTRA TRADERS, October 2004. SUMMERS ANTIQUES, proprietor Richard Millis, 2002-2004. Previously SEAFRESH FISHERIES, after being an empty lock-up shop for many years. BRAINS, butcher, 1986. H. INGRAM, meat purveyor, 1967-1973. LAURENCE J. BARTON, butcher 1959-1965. Mr DAPPS, butcher, circa 1911. Barbers Shop, 1905.

89. PEONY GARDENS, take-away Chinese food. 2003-2004. Formerly THOMPSONS take-away oriental foods. The RISING SUN chinese take-away, 1999. A teashop circa 1986 that closed about 1989. Formerly BRADFORD STORES, proprietor P. & F.J. Hoare, groceries and delicatessen, 1967-1977. ERNEST R. BRADFORD, grocer and provisions, 1959-1967. Mrs BRADFORD, confectioner, 1937.

91. HALIFAX BUILDING SOCIETY, estate agents, 1999-2004. Previously LEEDS BUILDINGS SOCIETY premises. SOUTHDOWN BUILDING SOCIETY. EASTBOURNE MUTUAL BUILDING SOCIETY, 1987. OUT OF TOWN BOUTIQUE, 1973-1977. POST OFFICE premises 1915-1967: Postmasters - J.H. Bonniface 1967, L.A. Walker 1965, Miss M. Bassett 1959. POST OFFICE, postmistress Miss I Godden, 1955, Miss Deeks, 1918-1946.

91a. PHILIP BASHAM, chiropodist, 1973.

Albert Place and some private houses.

95. HOMECARE EXTERIORS LOW MAINTENANCE PRODUCTS*. Proprietor David Tingley, 1997-2004. TAYLOR'S TIMBER MERCHANTS, garden centre 1972-1995. GARDEN CENTRE, proprietor E.S. Burt 1972-1973. GARDENCRAFT, 1959. Cornelius F. TAYLOR, carpenter, 1937.
In 1898 Cornelius P. Taylor organised a Cottage Gardners Show in Mr Diplocks Home Field. Corrie Taylor lived in Havelock House and later moved into WATKINS LAUNDRY where he had his business as carpenter and undertaker, 1932. Formerly Myrtonville Soft Water Laundry, 1918-1920, sometimes known as Mrs Mary Watkins laundry. Soft water was obtained from a large rainwater tank sunk below the floor, it was stated that 36 hand irons were in use at once. Sometimes known as Mertonville Soft Laundry. The property was occupied by Harry Streeter 1898-1899.
Possibly also the site of a workhouse. Location known as Watkin's Corner.

Top of High Street - Watkins Corner - junction with B2247 (old A27 pre 2003).

HIGH STREET - EVEN NUMBERS

MANOR PARK MEDICAL CENTRE, 1973-2004.
MANOR PARK COURT, Polegate Dental Practice, proprietor Dr N.J. Vaid, 1994-2004.
MANOR PARK PRACTICE, doctor's surgery, 2004.
MANOR PARK, estate agency, 1973.

St John's Road was originally named Station Road in 1846.

2. MIDLAND BANK, manager A.E. Parsloe, 1932-1937.

N.B. Nos 2 and 4 are actually now nos 12 and 14 High Street.

4. R.J. BLAND & SON, high class boot and shoe repairs, 1946-1957.

6. GABRIAL, ladies hairdresser, 1965. ARTHUR MILLS, chemist, 1937-1957. R.E. WALTER, fruiterer and greengrocer, Gilda Parade, 1955.

8. Private abode 2004. HAINE & SON, funeral directors, 1963-1977. ERNEST BRADFORD, grocer and taxi service, 1946. Mrs BRADFORD, grocer and confectioner, High Street, 1937.

In 1922 another shop was erected beside 12 High Street and re-numbered 14 High Street.

10. HELP THE AGED charity shop, 2004. Tim Smith ran this shop until his move across the road, to Nos 35/37, in 1994. JOHN ASHBY, grocer and provisions merchant, 1960-1991.

10a. J.F. ASHBY, 1973.

12. CHRISTIAN RESOURCE CENTRE, 2000-2004. FREDERICK S. HILL with family members, draper, shoes, and toys, 1919-1999. Proprietors: Daphne Pumfrey, daughter of Fred Hill 1955-1981. Pam Burton 1996-2002. Also the village Post Office 1900-1915. Previously known as 2 High Street. MIDLAND BANK 1932-1937. HARTE, READ, RIPPON & DODD, solicitors, 1955.

14. SLOANE'S SQUARE, newsagents and foodstuffs. Proprietor Ms Sloane Brodie, 2003-2004. CARTER'S NEWS 1996-2003. Previously BUCKLEY'S NEWS, 1976-1986, downstairs Brian and Annette Buckley created their Museum of Shops 1983-1986 that transferred to Battle High Street. RIVERSLEIGH, tea rooms and accommodation. N.C. DIBBLE, confectioner, 1963-1973. N. PHILLIPS, confectionery and tobacconist, 1959. Confectionery, bed and breakfast, Edwin Atkins, 1955. Pre 1922 as No 2 High Street: Mrs Stephens, 1921, Mrs Rogers,1918. As No 2 High Street in 1926 it was OLD MILL BAKERY of Wannock. Previously known as 4 High Street. R.J. BLAND, high class boot and shoe repairs, 1954-1957.

Black Path development and railway crossing.

16. Mrs E.C. STRUDWICK, 1967.

POLEGATE NURSING CENTRE, completed 1995.

18. Now car park to FORESTERS block of sixteen flats, built for New Downland Housing Association of Chichester.
Their car park plot built over site of original Junction Hotel 1850 and demolished 1975. Proprietors: Roland Luck 1967-1973, John Greig, 1967, George Thomas Atkins 1955, W.W. Watson 1935, Issac Valentine 1890-1899, Alexander Hurst 1882, Leonard Packham 1850. Also railway refreshment rooms, Dawson Davey's Eating House, Terminus Place 1899. The site of the Station Master's House, also Working Men's Club (1899).
The railway refreshment rooms were run by James Bradford 1899, run by Mrs Galdwin refreshment and level crossing 1899. Refreshment rooms proprietor Harriet Taylor 1887-1890. HORACE TAYLOR grocer and provisions 1887-1893.

Railway crossing.

Grassed plot now used as a town green was formerly the site of railway workers cottages, single storey booking office and goods sidings. The area now houses The Centre shops and offices above. With Keith Walton Newsagents backing the railway line and the third station, opened 1986, and booking office.

THE CENTRE. Opened August 1975.

1. MOBILITY PLUS, disability aids, 1998-2004. P. KEARNEY, builders and decorators, 1997-2003. Previously SCOTT'S INTERNATIONAL FLORISTS, 1980-1986.

2. CENTRE DRUG STORE, retailing domestic supplies, stationery etc, proprietor Councillor Christine Berry.

3. THRESHERS wine store, licensees M.M. Chappeau and V. Low. KEELING & SONS, wine merchants, 1986. Previously ROBERT'S OFF-LICENCE, the first occupier from 1975.

4. CARERS CORNER, charity shop, 2003-2004. Previously KITCHEN WORLD, kitchens and bathrooms, proprietors Marion and Mike Hyland, 2000. Formerly HOME PLANNING, kitchen units, 1980-1981.

5. POLEGATE FRUITERERS, greengrocers, proprietor Adrian Messenger, 2003-2004. POLEGATE FRUITERERS, proprietors Pat and Sue Brown, 1995.

6. THE MILL, cafe, proprietors Mike and Alison Steadman, 1986-2004, Hazel and Carlos 1987.

7. CO-OPERATIVE GROUP, supermarket 1997-2004. Licensees Rachel Cornell and Kim Ransley. During a £300,000 re-fit of the store it encompassed the main Post Office from 20.03.2003.

The shoppers car park area were railway sidings and the site of the Granary and Lamp House. In the car park was the REG SHINGLETON AMENITY CENTRE, for many years housing the Citizen's Advice Bureau and Youth Club was a porta cabin building that controversially was declared unsafe and demolished in 2000.

20. JOHN COWCHER, railway goods yard, 1967. D. CATT & SONS, corn merchants, 1967. A.W. SUTTON coal merchants 1967.

22. LAURENCE STREDWICK, 1967.

24. ALBERT SAYERS, 1967.

GILDA PARADE - now absorbed into High Street numeration.

1. RALPH FREEMAN, newsagent, 1946. HENRY THORNE, laundry, 1937.

2. R.E. WALTER, fruiterer and greengrocer, 1955.

3. A.G. BAKER, outfitter, 1937.

4. Mrs LEILA HARRIS, ladies and gents hairdresser, 1946. Miss D.F. BOND, hairdresser, 1937.

5. THE GEM, proprietors: Eric Brown 1938, William Morris, stationer and toys 1946-1955. ERIC TURNER, confectioner, 1937.

6. Mrs M. JESSUP, greengrocer and fruiterer, 1937-1946. Edward Venn, physician and surgery, 1946.

7. EAST SUSSEX RADIO, wireless engineers, 1955.

8. GILDA CAFE, proprietor Mrs Meads, 1955. COOMBES BROS, cycle dealers, 1937.

9. J.J. SMITHSON, fried fish shop, 1946.

10. C.F. TAYLOR, hairdresser, 1955

11. FLORENCE, Mrs F. Willis, 1946. Mrs F. WALLIS, draper, 1946.

HIGH STREET continued

30. J. TOLHURST, wholesale confectioner. 1967.

32-34. POLEGATE PETS*, proprietor Sadde Trust, 2004. Previously FAIRWAYS HARDWARE, proprietors Lynda and Derek Davies 1981-2003. Previously owned by Susie and Nick Penny 1983. Previously owned by Pam and John Hollingsworth for some ten years. Formerly ASHERS HARDWARE, ironmongery and gardens, 1970-1973. COSTON'S HARDWARE, IRONMONGERS, 1965-1967 GILDA HARDWARE, proprietor R.A. Byewater, 1965.

34. C.M. BEDFORD-TURNER, physician and surgeon, with Joseph Moran, 1973. JOSEPH MORAN, physician and surgeon, 1967-1973.

36-38. DEAN TANDOORI*, restaurant, proprietors, Mary and Abdul Hashim, 2000- 2004 also BANGLATOWN, same owners 2000. VILLAGE CAFE, 1994-1997. HALL second hand furniture and removals 1981-2001. FLEETLINE radio cars, 1981. TAYLOR'S FRUIT, 1973. GILDA DOMESTIC STORES, proprietor Richard Bywater, 1959-1967. TOLHURST, confectionery, 1959.

38. DEAN TANDOORI, 2003-2004. POLEGATE VIDEO PLUS*, proprietors Roger White and Jon Murrell 1992-2001. HALL second hand furniture and removals 1981-2001. POLY CLEAN, launderette, 1973. W.J. BRACEY & SON, grocers, 1965. W.J. BRACEY, grocers and provisions, 1959.

40. SNACK ATTACK, take-away foods, 2003-2004. POLEGATE KEBAB SHOP, 1998. ABBIE'S CORNER, bakery and cafe, 1995. J.W.M. SMITH, confectionery, 1973. J.H. HEASEMAN, confectioner, 1965-1967. THE GEM, Tricia and Ray Sorrell. 1955-1986. WILLIAM MORRIS, confectionery, 1959. ERIC TURNER, confectioner, 1937. THE CAFE, 1935.

GILDA CRESCENT.

42. DIRECT TRAVEL TAXIS, 1996-2004. POLEGATE INFORMATION CENTRE, for about one year. GREENGROCERS proprietors Jim and wife 1985. BRIAN AND PAM'S, fruit and groceries, 1977. Formerly R.E. WALTER, fruiterer and florist, 1968-1970. LINDSAY'S FRUIT, 1973. GILDA HARDWARE STORES, proprietor R.A. Bywater, 1960-1963. R.E. WALTER, fruiterer and grocer, 1959-1967. GILDA DOMESTIC STORES, proprietor George Ward, 1954-1957. JESSOPS GREEN GROCERS.

42a L.GIBBONS 1973.

44. THE QUILT BOX, joint proprietors Sophie Hay and Tracey Parks, opened September 2000. Previously MA LARKINS, grocers, proprietor Amanda Buck, 2003. TRITECH, computers, videos and television, 1999. POLEGATE T.V. AND VIDEO, 1997. SUSSEX COUNTY BUILDING SOCIETY, 1986. LEWES BUILDING SOCIETY, 1973. EAST SUSSEX RADIO, domestic electrical goods and bicycles, 1957-1967.

46. ROWLAND SMITH, accountants, proprietor Mike Smith, 2004. HOGARTH BUSINESS SERVICES, 1995-1996. NEW GILDA CAFE, proprietor G.G. Maynard, 1959-67. Formerly MELANIE'S RESTAURANT, proprietor Geoffrey Maynard, 1954.

48. ARCHER & PARTNERS*, estate agents, Graham Archer and David Sheldon, 2001-2004. HOUSE & MORTGAGE CENTRE, 1999. Previously HALIFAX BUILDING SOCIETY. Formerly BALCH & CO, estate agents, 1967-1986. ALFRED SAYERS, fishmonger, 1965.

50. CHAP'S BARBERS, gentlemen's hairdressers, 2002-2004. Formerly FAIRDEAL TRAVEL. C.F. TAYLOR, gentlemen's hairdresser, proprietor Charles Taylor, 1959-1973.

52. KAO WAH, chinese take-away food 1986-2004. Previously KAY'S ladies and children's wear, wools and haberdashery, dry cleaning, 1967, proprietors Daisy Chick and her husband T. Chick, 1957-1973. Formerly JOHN & JANE drapers, ladies wear and library, 1954.

52a. Mrs E.E. JOY, toys and radio engineers, a wooden timber frame workshop set down from the yard outside, 1934-1946. Site of present public conveniences, formerly site of stables to Polegate Inn.

54. DINKUM, public house, licensee J. Shoesmith. Re-named THE DINKUM 1979 during extensive renovation of the frontal appearance. It was proposed to move the front aspect back 16 feet, to align with other properties and move the front door to the side, but only the latter happened. See photos on page 89. POLEGATE INN, 1855-1979. Previously known as The RAILWAY ARMS 1847, owned by Harvey's of Lewes since 1847 - prior to which it may have been a beer house.

The building of shops known as 56-58b were on land previously occupied by a smithy, blacksmith and workshop owned by Owen Crowhurst in the 1800s. Smithy buildings 1840-1965. Latterly Handford's Taxis. Traded by William Wood, harness maker and wheelwright who died in 1934, although his name carried on at the site. Also occupied as Waghorn's garage, petrol pumps at the premises. T.R LARKIN, saddler, 1918.

56. CO-OP FUNERALCARE, 1998-2004. Previously a wholesale jewellry facility, briefly also a stationery shop? 1995. DURNFORD SMITH, solicitors, 1993. KEYMARKETS, grocers. QUALITY FAIR, grocers, 1973.

56a. FOX & SON, estate agents, manager Rob Rann, 1998-2004. HOLMES & LEADBITTER, estate agents, 1986. PARTON & CO, estate agents, Thomas MacKellar, 1983. Formerly BEX TELEVISION CENTRE, 1970-1972. A modern block of flats and retail outlets built on this site in the 1960s. Previously at this location was a property named The Cottage and in 1909 as Station House.

58. BEEJAY CARPETS, proprietor Bruce Tarrant, 1984-2004. A.J. FABRICS, proprietors John and Edna Shewring, curtain and dress materials, 1981-1983. D. & F. ATHERALL, furnishing boutique, 1973.

58a BARRACLOUGH, STILES & PARTNERS, opticians, 1996-2004. Formerly DOROTHY WALTERS, ladies fashions, house of fashion, proprietor Miss Patricia Reader 1981-1983, Toni Greenway 1972-1983, Mrs D. Ogden, 1970.

58b. CARERS CORNER, charity shop, 2002-2004. P. KEARNEY, builder and decorator, 1997. POLEGATE BAKERS, 1981. Formerly occupied by CHARLOTTES, ladies wear. MOBILITY PLUS, mobility aids, 1977. CHICKEN & HERWOOD, builders, 1973. C. & S. TOYS & SPORT, 1970-1073.

On a grass verge on the north side of this block of shops for many years had rested the Liberty Stone. The centuries old edifice - five feet tall by two foot wide in chert stone - was a boundary marker of the ancient liberty of Pevensey. The stone had been carelessly removed in January 1968 by contractors working on the new block of flats and retail units. At first the local press reported that the stone had been dumped on the Crumbles wasteland near Eastbourne. Eventually Parish Clerk Ben Hick was able to determine that the stone had in fact been dumped in a 12 foot deep pond at Firle. However it remained there due to the prohibitive cost of any removal plans.

72. G.P.O. POST OFFICE and sorting room, 1967 to 20.03.2003. B. & Q. POST OFFICE 1973. Mrs L.A. CROWHURST, 1973. The property was constructed with 30 feet deep foundations to bear a proposed second floor, that has never been built. POST OFFICE customer services re-located in the Co-op Store during 2003, sorting office remained behind the empty Post Office premises.
Built on previously open land known as Daveys Field that had been occupied as an AA gun post in WWII.

ALBERT ROAD

Here stood Osborne House - one of the communities most noble homes in grandiose Italianate style akin to Queen Victoria's Isle of Wight retreat. Built for William Henry Attwood, his home was demolished in 1962 and the present block of flats were erected. Osborne House was occupied in 1955 by the Maitland family and the last occupants were a family named Curran. The property appeared in a 1925 auction catalogue offered by Powell & Co of Hailsham . . . at a very low reserve. Present bungalow no 18 built in 1962 on site of Mr Attwood's former Roman Catholic chapel.

5. Built over in 1987 as Chiltern Court, block of eight flats. A modest bungalow, and small holding, appropriately named Winsome, previously occupied the plot. Built in 1925 it was first prize in a TiT Bits magazine Bullets competition won by a Mr Holt. Details of the property appear in a 1927 auction catalogue.

Numbers **7-15** were built by Henry Twine, also the bungalow no. 24.

18. 1962 bungalow built by Eastbourne builders Miller & Selms, for Maurice Beck, a Polegate electrician.

20-22. No 22 named as Sunnyside. This pair of detached houses are shown of the official 1873 map. An early occupant was Mrs Shoesmith. The property has been occupied as GPO TELEPHONE EXCHANGE. The right hand ground floor property housed the manual telephone equipment and the first floor was occupied by Dave Williams the telephone superintendent, 1977. A school run by Miss Dapps occupied the ground floor of the left hand side property, 1955. Telephone Exchange, 1937. Stables to the rear were utilised as garages for GPO vehicles. 1929-1934: an employee named Mrs Muriel Randall was employed here as Telephonist/Caretaker and her family may have lived there also.

29. H.G PARSONS & SON, plastering contractors, 1965.

32. HENRY TWINE, builder, 1955.

BLACK PATH
Forester House flats completed in 1998 for New Downland Housing Association of Chichester. The road being unmade for many years merely as a track running parallel to the railway line between stations. Previously the site of the original Junction Hotel of 1850.

POLEGATE NURSING CENTRE, completed 1995.

BROAD ROAD
16. THE VALLEY CAR HIRE SERVICE, proprietor G.M. FIELD, 1959-1967.

68. SUSSEX GARAGE DOORS, 2003. KIDMAN'S GROCERY, provisions, 1965-1967. L.S. JONES, provisions, 1957.

70. DENTAL SURGERY, 2002-2004.

St Wilfrid's Church built in 1961.

BROOK STREET.
First laid out and built upon as artisans dwellings 1868-1890.

2. JESSE PAGE, baker 1935-1946. J. PAGE, baker, 1932.

3. Depot for C.W. ROSE & SON 1965-1967. W.H. APPLIN, builders, 1964. Rear of No 3 - E.J. PHAROAH, plant hire.

3a. TOM BLOORE MOTORS, engineers, 1977-2004. Previously SPOONERS, vehicle workshops that included the Listed slaughter house premises, including outhouses that were partially demolished in 1981.

4. S.B. TAYLOR, London House, grocer, 1921-1937. LONDON SUPPLY STORES, Arthur Weller, then W.H. Laurence, 1918-1932. WILLIAM PIPER, painter, 1899. Mrs MARY ANN TAYLOR, grocer, 1890.

5. MAURICE WOOD, dairyman, 1955-1959.

6. POLEGATE TELEVISION, 1967. S.B. TAYLOR, grocer and provisions, 1955-1959. Now a rendered private abode. Samuel Taylor opened his grocers stores in 1868 and it remained in business for about seventy years. SAMUEL BERTRAM TAYLOR, London House grocer, 1921-1937. WILLIAM COLBRAN, florist, 1890.

8. JAMES TOLHURST, baker and grocer, 1918. See also Cross Street material. JESSE PAGE, baker and confectioner, 1959.

9. N.L. CROUCH, landscape gardener, 1980.

11. BENJAMIN BONIFACE, fishmonger, 1937, property now demolished. JAMES ATTRELL, bookmaker, 1924.

6. OWEN CROWHURST, blacksmith, 1899.

15/17 and 25. Residences marked with CD 1903 foundation stones - query Caleb Diplock connections - possibly occupied by his employees, with ease of access across the brook to Southdown Hall opposite.

WILLIAM WOOD haulage contractor 1955. Works depot and coal yard, William Wood built a modern house for his wife Ida in front of the yard.

32 32. WILLIAM SKINNER, chimney sweep, 1927.

45. J. & G. HOLTER, bootmaker, 1920-1937.

Private homes numbers 48-72 are headed Clifton Terrace.

CHURCH ROAD
T. LEACH, Burlington Nursery, 1921-1935. Site was previously known as Burlington Gates.
CHURCH ROAD NURSERIES, proprietors Mrs B.C. Gaut, C.B. Spooner, William Gaut, 1955-1968.

6. HARRY R. VINE, Fourways, carpenter and joiner, 1970.

CROSS STREET
M.E. COLEMAN/BEX ELECTRICAL, TV engineers, repairs to cassettes, radios etc, 1980.
MANKTELOW, upholsterer, 1965-1967.
H.R. VINE, carpenter's workshops, 1973.

1. LESLIE TOOKEY, monumental mason, 1947-2004.

2. BROOKS CARPETS, 2004. Briefly TRIANGLE FENCING SUPPLIES, 2003. Previously PARTCO AUTOPARTS, vehicle trade parts suppliers, 1973-2000. PIGGOTT CONFECTIONERY, 1967. J. TOLHURST, wholesale confectionery, proprietor E.W. Ward, 1955. TOLHURST confectionery manufacturers once occupied premises at no 6, a former bakery facing no 2. TOLHURST, confectionery manufacturers, proprietor B.R. Smith, 1946. In the late 1950s Tolhurst operated from a brick faced building on former railway land as no 36 High Street, where The Drug Store now stands in The Centre. Cross Street site also as A.G. MARTIN, wholesale confectioner, 1937.

4. POLEGATE SECURITY, storage for Priceguard Locksmiths, 2004.

5. JAMIE WOOD, bird cages 1973-2000 - property burnt down 2000 and became numbers 5 & 5a private residences. Also JAMIE'S TOYS, toy manufacturers, 1967.

DITTONS ROAD & CHAUCER INDUSTRIAL ESTATE.
DITTONS STORE, proprietors C. &. E. Briant, groceries and provisions, 1963.
Unit 7, MAYNARDS CATERING, Proprietors Alison and Richard Packham 1990-2004. Geoffrey Maynard, 1996.
Unit 9. TYRES, alloy wheel and tyre specialists, 2003.
EAST SUSSEX GROWERS, horticultural, 1973.
PIGGOTT CONFECTIONERY 1973.
FARGRO, horticultural sundriesman, 1973.
WHITE SWAN GARAGE, motor sales, 1997-2004. Previously DITTONS ROAD FILLING STATION. 1995.
WATERHOUSE COACHES, Robin Bank, Dittons Road, proprietor Keith Waterhouse, 1967-2003. Edward Waterhouse, 1973. R.D. RANDALL, carriers, 1959. TWINE'S BUSES, Henry Twine, 1930.
BRAMLEY NURSERIES, Dittons Road, 1973.
W.G. KOCH, nurserymen, Dittons Nursery, 1973.
BASIL KING, Bramley Nursery, 1973.
HENRY LOVEGROVE, Bramley Nursery, 1973.

CHAUCER INDUSTRIAL ESTATE.
Unit One. Sutch Printers (Polegate) Ltd, 1975.
Unit Two: John Botting Antiques, 1975.
Unit Three: Anglian Windows Ltd, 1975.
Unit Four: Graham Price Antiques (A27), 1975.
Unit Five: Clavering Organics Real Gardening Ltd, 1975.
Unit Six: J.J. Adam (Haulage) Ltd, 1975.
Unit Seven: A27 Antiques, 1975.
Unit Eight: Angears Ltd. 1975. Angears, confectionery makers established in Herstmonceux 40 years ago, closed in August 1986 with the loss of 40 jobs. The unit had been bought by Rank Hovis McDougall who then bought the Piggotts factory in Polegate. The Rank concern had sold the business to the 1986 owners four years previously. Units Eight and Nine became part of Britannia Superfine Ltd, confectionery manufacturers.
Unit Nine: Starpack Freezers Ltd and Starpack Frozen Foods Ltd, 1975.
British Antiques Warehouse opened on the estate in June 1982 with five directors, the trio of British partners being John Botting, Graham Price and Lloyd Williams.

Current businesses a Chaucer Industrial Estate.
Trade & Save Vehicles.
Unit One: G.C.G. Engineering Co.
Unit Three: Akro Valve Ltd.
Unit Four: Office & Reception Planters.
Unit Five: Airles Systems.
Electro Diamond Services.
Weatherlux Ltd.
Tyres Direct.
Coastline Windows.
Gas Plus Technical Services.
Hammond.
Glasline Quality Sealed Units.
Britannia Superfine Ltd.
EDF Energy plc Waste Transfer.

DITTONS CORNER
The first brick was laid on new large estate at Dittons Corner in early October 1962, construction being undertaken by Laing Builders. The estate was to comprise of 134 bungalows and chalets, sending the estimated population of Polegate over the 6,000 mark.

DOVER ROAD AREA
Levett Builders erected all the bungalows between Dover Road and Levett Road (numbers 57-87) except for the bungalow at the very top of the service road which was built on Mr Scrase's land by an unknown builder many years after the war. All this construction work was done before the outbreak of war in 1939.
The land was used for agricultural needs until 1956 when G. Levett Co were allowed to re-start building the Levett Estate between 1956 and 1963. Dymchurch Close, Rye Close, Shepham Lane and Glynleigh were built by Farnham Building Estate Agents 1960-1970. The rest of the estate was constructed by Gilbert Levett.

EASTBOURNE ROAD
Polegate's first set of traffic lights, at the A22 crossroads, were officially put into operation by the area Ministry of Transport Officer on November 30th 1964. In May 1986 plans to install traffic lights at the junction of the A22 and A27 Lewes Road met opposition from town councillors. They feared that the town's already worsening vehicle problems would be compounded by a build up of through traffic.

TESCO EXPRESS STORES & ESSO SERVICE STATION, 1988-2004. Tesco Express store opened July 9th 2001. June 1988 a new canopy was completed, three weeks ahead of schedule, over a re-vamped garage forecourt. The site had been cleared and re-developed in 17 weeks and cost £500,000. Previous garage closed September 10th 1987 for refurbishment. The proprietor remained as Brian Petch who had taken over from his father the late Eric Petch who died in 1969. POLEGATE MOTOR CO, BMC and Rover dealers and engineers, service station 1937-1973. BEN WEISS MOTORS circa 1954. Also site of HILL & Co TOOLS. MANSFIELDS Ltd, motorists services 1946. COUNTY SERVICE STATION 1932-1935.

14. BLACK & WHITE TAXIS and self-drive hire, J.A. Barnard, 1965-1967 and A.G. Bowes, Marian Lodge, 1965.

27. DOWNLAND HOMESTEADS, estate agents and valuers, partner Joe Tumbrell, 1965-1967.

96. THE SNACK BOX. George Weisse, The Snack Box, refreshment rooms 1946-1959.

205. Dr L.L. BANKS, surgery, 1965.

251. OMEGA, building works, 1999.

FARMLANDS WAY. Mill stream flows under Farmlands Way.
39. SUSSEX GARAGE DOORS, 2004. V.L. CROFTS, wine and spirit merchants, 1967-1973. D. & M. FOSTER, grocers, 1967.

41. WANNOCK POST OFFICE & NEWSAGENTS*, proprietors Jean and Brian Temple, 1991-2004. R. &.R. ALLADICE, newsagents and sub-Post Office, 1973. L.&.B. LEGATE, news and Post Office, 1967. W.A. GASKIN, newsagents, 1965.

43. WOODWARD ELECTRICAL & SECURITY, 2004. D. & M. FOSTER, grocery and provisions, 1967. A.E. GOACHER, grocer, 1965.

45. Unoccupied, 2004. TRADITIONS, furniture, 2003. ASHER'S HARDWARE, pet foods etc, 1997-1980. J.H. WATERHOUSE, hardware dealers, 1967.

Big Sofa Shop Ltd, in Farmlands Way, went into compulsory liquidation on October 29th 2001.

GRAND PARADE.
1. COLVILL CLEANING, commercial services, 2004. BUSTINS, newsagents, 1973-2000. KEELEY'S, newsagent and mini market, 1999. E.J.N. CURTIS, newsagent and confectioner, 1951-1976. EDWIN FREEMAN, newsagent, 1946.

2. WILLINGDON PLUMBING & HEATING. THE RADIATOR CENTRE*, proprietor Brian Nesbit. 2002-2004. POST OFFICE & STORES, 1995. POST OFFICE & STORES, proprietor B. Williams, also Mrs K.E. Williams, Post Office and grocer, 1946-1967.

3. WASHETERIA, self-service launderette, 1967-2004. Miss DOROTHY GARDINER and MRS W. GARDINER, upholsterers, 1946-1955.

4. GALLERY 4*, picture framing and art gallery, proprietor David Reed. 1988-2004. Previously an engraver and chronologist workshop, 1987. KINGSTON FLOOR & WALL TILING, 1976. L.M. FARNHAM, surveyors, auctioneers and valuers, 1959-1965. Mrs Fox and WILLIAM BEETLESTONE draper, 1951.

5. VICEROY restaurant, 1999-2004. formerly DEAN TANDOORI, proprietors Mary and Abdul Hashim. R.D. RANDALL, hardware, 1967. H.W. SMITH, hardware, 1965. J.&G. TURNER, hardware, 1959. William Saunders, DELANEY'S HARDWARE, 1951. C.F. SIMMONS, Cowley's Dairies, 1946.

6. ANN TAYLOR, Mrs T. White, ladies hairdresser, 1946.

6a. Joseph Rodgers, 1951.

7. Mrs ELIZABETH SCHLUMPF, baker, 1946.

6-7. THOROUGHBRED public house, proprietor Ruth Weisham, 2003. Extensive building extensions to the eastern side of the building, doubling it's size, were completed during 2000. This block now headed Accommodation and Function Room. Previously THE MERRY WIFES', a Romanesque format wine bar, proprietor Michael Crosbie. Formerly THE BEEHIVE, proprietor Edward Coates to 1980. TUDOR CAFE, proprietor C. Callan 1951. Youth Club founded by Geoffrey Maynard, 1951-1973.

GOLDEN MILLER LANE
30. HARRY WEAVERS, teacher of music, 1955.

HAILSHAM ROAD.
A.F. COOPER, general stores, 1932.
CHARLES WOOD, beekeeper, Rosebank, 1955.
R.A. & W. WAITES, Yorkshire Pantry cafe, 1955-1967.
HONEY CRAG, 2000, access off Hailsham Road, previously Hither Gate, Butlers chicken farm.

4-4a. Approximate site of the Toll House built around 1785 and demolished in 1910. Also known as Swine's Hill Gate. Around 1936-1937 single house was built for Dr J. Martin and called Tussocks. Harry Dodd, 1955, later converted to a pair of semi-detached houses known as 4 and 4a. Numbers 2-2a were built postwar.

5. STEPHEN RIGSBY, double glazing etc, 1999.

5a. THE CORNERSTONE - SEVENTH DAY ADVENTIST CHURCH. 2000-2004. MENCAP, charity centre, 1979, closed 31.01.91. COUNTY PRIMARY SCHOOL, infants 1967. Built 1850 as a church school.

7. Site of old brickfields.

9. HEATHER BANK, C.W. Rose & Son, decorators, plumbers and builders 1918-1970.

Houses at 9 and 11 were built in 1893 by Mr Rose.

15. DOVE brides dress hire, 2004. Previously MONTAGUE ANTIQUES, proprietors Tina and Hans Seringer, 1998. MONTAGUE STORES, grocers, proprietor Mrs P.G. Small, 1965-1967: originally owned by Allen Montague. J.G. REEVE, drug stores, 1935. Montague Villa was built in 1879.

CUPRESSUS NURSERY, proprietors Elizabeth and Douglas Reeve, 1935-1973. The nursery was sold-off to make way for Queensmead Residential Home, built 1987-1988, and opened in May 1989. Frontage is in Victoria Road as no 84.

49-61. Plot of ALBION NURSERY 1977, No 61 occupied as V.F. GODDARD & SON, nurserymen in 1967. GODDARD & SON, nurserymen, Albion Nursery 1955. The cottages on this site and the nursery were sold to Guardian Royal Insurance Co who demolished the cottages and built the flats known as Guardian Court.

74. EAST SUSSEX CONSTABULARY. 1955-1965.

HONEYCRAG CLOSE

9. JUDITH DUNSMORE, therapeutic cushions, 1999. Former site of Herbert Butler's Chicken Farm, Hither Gate, 1935 - accessed from Hailsham Road. Private homes built here in 1990s.

LEVETT ROAD

Levett builders built all the bungalows between Dover Road and Levett Road (numbers 57-87) except for the bungalow at the very top of the service road which was built on Mr Scrace's land by an unknown builder many years after the war. All this construction work was done before the outbreak of war in 1939.

The land was used for agricultural needs until 1956 when G. Levett Co were allowed to re-start building Levett Estate between 1956 and 1963.

MANOR PARK ESTATE

Built by Bruce Margrett Co., who it is said went into liquidation.

MILLFIELDS, STATION ROAD

Millfields Farm/Swine's Hill. Farmhouse demolished in 1957, had been in existence in 1842 and extended in 1855. Bungalow numbered 9 occupies site of former farmhouse.

1. HIGHCROFT VETERINARY SURGERY, 2004. BASIL DEAN, bakery on site, 1973. DUNCAN FOSTER, bakers, 1965-1967. C. TOWNSEND, bakery at rear on current parking lot, 1937-1959.

2. KONTOUR CYCLES, 1997-2004. FREEDOM BIKES, 1995. TAGGS newsagents, Mr & Mrs R.W. Tagg, 1982. THE TIMES NEWSAGENTS/CHESHIRE'S Newsagents, Graham and Angela Cheshire, 1981 to August 1982. FIELDERS NEWSAGENT 1977? N.S. PIPER, newsagent, 1975. MILLFIELD NURSERY, 1973. W.H. SMITH, newsagents, 1956-1967. R.T. FOTHERLY, electrical engineer, 1946. C. TOWNSEND, baker, 1946. JOY'S ELECTRIC, electrical contractors, 1937.

3. POLEGATE SADDLERY*. Proprietors Mr R.C. Streeter and Mrs J. Streeter, 1982-2004. F.S.L. SADDLERY 1977. THRESHERS WINES, proprietors Herbert White and Fred Summerfield, 1973. FINDLATER MACKIE, PRENTIS, wine & spirit merchants, 1959-1967. W.H. SMITH, newsagents and stationers, 1957. H. DUFFIELD, newsagents and confectionery, 1954. W. MILLAR, stationer, 1937.

4. PROLIFIC PLUMBING & HEATING, 2004. MICHAEL, ladies hair stylist, Michael Peeling, 1965-1998. Formerly LEONARD G. COX, ladies hairdresser, 1959-1997. GILDA SALOON hairdressers with Leonard G. Cox, 1954-1957. Miss E. LEWIN, fancy draper, also as No 7, 1937-1946.

NEW ROAD
J.A. BARNARD, New Road Garage, paraffin oil distributor, 1959-1965.
SELVEY BROTHERS, market gardeners, (1955).
17 New Road was once 3 Noakes Cottages.
The location of Noakes Cottages built circa 1900. In 1964 Leslie Slevey, a gardener of 7 Noakes Cottages, sold a corner plot of land to William Applin & Co. This plot was divided into two parcels of land and in 1965 William Applin Co built a detached house for his daughter who was married to a railway signalman. The frontage is in the current Westfield Close, the remainder of the properties formed part of New Road and were re-numbered.

NURSERY CLOSE
Private abodes built by Maurice Levett builders in the 1930s.

OTHAM COURT
The property and grounds were acquired several years ago by the Ministry of Transport as part of the A27 bypass plans. The last owner being Ed Bicknell, best known as the manager of Dire Straits pop group. The site has a resident cartetaker and reportedly sold for £1m in August 2004.

OLD DRIVE
Private homes were built on the grounds of the former Southdown Hall from the early 1950s.
VOYCE DECORATORS, CORNER, 10 Old Drive, 1999.

PEVENSEY ROAD
H. CUSDIN, Hillcrest Nurseries, 1935.
SOUTHLANDS ESTATE OFFICE, 1937.
W. TURNER, general stores, 1935.
Numbers 1,3, 5. are named Queen Anne's Villas.
No 25 Fellands built by Gilbert Levett in 1933 and occupied by his widow and family members to 1999. Frontage extended unfortunately.
G. Levett builders constructed Nursery Close and along Pevensey Road until the war stopped building work. The land was used for agricultural needs until 1956 when G. Levett Co were allowed to re-start building Levett Estate between 1956 and 1963.

1. ROBIN SHEPPARD, plumbing, 1996-2004.
17. POLEGATE TAXI & CAR HIRE SERVICE, proprietor W. Hanks, 1935-1972.
21. Cran-lea private abode built for Sarah Colbran/Andrews after her husband died in 1927.
23. Private abode built for a Mrs Glazebrook.
25. Fellands private abode built by Maurice Levett builders in 1933.
27, 29, 31 private abodes built by Maurice Levett builders in mid 1930s.
55. CASSIES'S CAR HIRE SERVICE, 1963.
81. RICHARD SIMON ENTERPRISES, proprietor Simon Tanner, blinds, curtains and home maintenance, 1999.
2. POLLY ARCH. Joseph Ripley, scrap metal etc, 1973.

SAYERLAND ROAD.
The majority of the mid 1960s Sayerland estate bungalows are Wichello built.
A. HINTON, general stores, 1937.
RAYMOND WOOD, farmer, New Barn and Bramley Farms, 1955.

3. D.&.A. SKINNER, carpenters and builders, 1986.

27. LESLIE CROUCH, wood merchant, 1965.

127. MICHAEL CLARKE, scrap metal dealer. In 2002 the property was demolished to make way for the A27 bypass. L. CROUCH, scrap metal merchants, 1973.

SAYERLAND LANE.
WORCESTER & SON, builders, The Martlets, Sayerland Lane.

SCHOOL LANE
A proposal by developer Henry Twine, who lived close-by at the corner with Station Road, was placed with Hailsham Rural Council to create a petrol filling station at a new 350 homes estate road off School Lane. In December 1964 Polegate Parish Council voted in favour of the plan adjoining four (new) shops 200 yards down School Lane. Fortunately this development never took place. The Council also considered outline proposals for the Millfields block of homes and retail units at this time.

STATION ROAD
E.J. Le GRYS, general stores, 1932-1935.
SELVEY BROTHERS, market gardeners, 1955.
W.H. SMITH & SON, newsagents, Polegate Station No 2, 1955.
T.&E. VERRELL, general shop, 1935-1937. T.J. VERRELL, hairdresser, 1918.
WISSAM & SON, bootmakers, 1918-1935.

1. & 10. MORGAN & MORGAN, drapers, 1918-1937.

5. WILLIAM MILLAR, newsagent and wines, 1946.

10. Mrs M. TURNER, baker, 1935-1937. T.J. WENHAM, furniture brokers and dealers, 1924.

11. A.J. HELSDON, grocer, 1937.

13. HENRY TWINE, builder, 1959-1973.

49. PRISTINE SERVICES, offices, 2004. SANDELLS MAINTENANCE, building works, 1999. E.J. and HETTY BRADFORD, fruiterer and tobacconist,1946-1973.

61. M.D.GATES, coal merchants, 1960-1965. E. HAROLD GATES, coal merchants, also at Pevensey Road, 1946.

66-78. Six private terraced homes, known as Railway Cottages. Polegate Arbour in the 1930s has been recalled behind Railway Terrace, where horses and livestock were unloaded from the trains.

67. POLEGATE INSURANCE SERVICES, Tony Blunden, 1986-2004. H. WARD, baker, 1959. M. TURNER & SONS, bakers, 1946.

69. ANSOWER CLOTHING*/ ANSOWER TRADING CO. Proprietor Patrick Reed, garment manufacturing offices, 1998-2004. Previously APPLE WINDOWS, 1993-1998. HALLMARK, double-glazing showrooms, 1993. WATERHOUSE, green grocer, 1973. F.J. BENNETT, general store, 1967. G.C. WINTER, grocer, 1962-1963. HAROLD WARD, general stores, 1946.

71. KEN'S NEWSAGENTS, 1996-2004. MY WOOL SHOP, 1973. F.J. REEVE, draper, 1965-1967. POLEGATE SUPPLIES, gas stoves, 1959.

76. GATES, builders, 2 Railway Cottages, 1999.

81. M.D. GATES & CO., coal and haulage, 1965.

93. G. WORCESTER, builders, 1967.

97. CROSS CHANNEL MOTORCYCLES, 2004 previously SPUD'S MOTORCYCLES, 2003. JUNCTION STORES run by Paulene and as POLEGATE TAXI SERVICE undertaken by John - date uncertain. JUNCTION STORES, proprietor W. Knight, general groceries, 1957-1973. C.R MAYGLOTHING, grocer, 1965-1967. W. KNIGHT, grocer and general stores, 1959. GEORGE KENNARD, grocers, 1946. H. PRATT (died 1935) , grocers, 1909-1935. JUNCTION STORES, (1905).

JUNCTION INN - built 1882 by Hurst & Cardwell, later the Star Brewery. Known by this name in 1930. Currently owned by Greene King group - licencees Kenneth Stanley Castell and Moira Castell. Junction Tavern proprietors Brenda and Ian Freshwater 1999-2001, Isaac Valentine 1887-1899, Charles Smith 1882 - now titled The Junction.

101. POLEGATE ANGLING CENTRE, 1986-2004. PAT & JOHN'S FLOWERS, garden centre, 1973-1976. HOME & GARDEN CENTRE, hardware, 1965-1967. H.S. KIBBLEWHITE, hardwear, 1959. MORGAN & MORGAN, drapers, 1902-1946. SAMUEL TAYLOR, OUTFITTERS & SHOES, 1882.

105. POLEGATE TAXI SERVICES. E.A. Parsons, 1967. POLEGATE TAXI SERVICE, Proprietor Capt Jack Handford, late Bradford's, 1957-1970: proprietor F.A. Parsons, 1965-1968.

Railway Station, second site, 1880-1986. Currently BUDDIES AT OLD POLEGATE STATION, restaurant. Previously BREWERS FAYRE. Location of KEITH'S bookstall 1977. W.H. SMITH & SON, newsagents 1955-1967. KEITH WALTON next at current station as K. WALTON, railway station newsagent. 1980-2004.

ST JOHN'S ROAD

POLEGATE Nurseries, W.D. Elder, 1921-1932.
E. RANDALL, carriers, Marlowes Lodge, 1935.

St John's Church constructed in 1874. In 1893 a small lending library was operated from the Vestry, wherein books were allocated each Friday at a half penny. The church hall was built in 1960.

17. Mrs H. BAILLIE, school, 1946.

41. ST JOHN'S NURSERIES, proprietor Capt G.H. Boultbee-Whall, 1932-1965.

45. THOMPSON'S NURSERIES, 1967-1973. G. THOMPSON & SONS, 1955-1965. ST JOHN'S NURSERIES, 1954-1963. Proprietor: Capt G.H. Boultbee-Whall, 1935.

67. TURNER'S (POLEGATE), bakers, 1955.

REDCROFT. Built 1881 - derelict 2004 awaiting site re-development. As RED HOUSE in 1967 occupied by Horace W. Tiddenham. In the 1940s it was the retirement home of the Vicar of Polegate Rev. A.C.H. Black, 1937. Edward Apps, 1932. Simon Saxon, 1918. Edward Radfor, 1909. Edward B. Ryder, 1894-1895.

August 2004. Bulldozers looked set to make way for new homes lodged by local developer St Mary's Homes. The plan is to demolish forelorn Red Croft and erect two blocks of four one-bedroomed flats and four two-bedroomed flats. Another pair of two-bedroomed cottages and a bungalow along with a new access road are envisaged. Planning applications were first made ten years ago. Red Croft's former owner went to America in the 1960s and left the house in the care of a neighbour, who passed way - leaving his family to take responsibility of the property. Late September 2004. Best Demolition Co moved onto the plot and started lifting tiles and other building salvage material and clearing the site.

ST LEONARD'S ROAD
St Leonard's Laundry was demolished in 1975 and the site was re-developed with new homes.
St Leonard's Nurseries, Thomas Allen, 1927.

ST JOHN'S ROAD.
G. THOMPSON & SONS, Polegate Nurseries, 1955.

5. **FREDERICK STEPHENS**, decorator, Ivydene, 1955.

20. Built in 1894 and occupied by Pearl and Peter Field since 1969 as a Bed and Breakfast facility.

45. THOMPSON'S NURSERIES, 1973. St JOHN'S NURSERIES, cut flowers and floral designs, 1954-1963.

STUD FARM ESTATE
The 8th Duke of Devonshire established a horse breeding and training stables and named it Stud Farm, after his death it was briefly owned by Solly Joel the diamond mine investor. The Mile Oak Development Co, of Portslade, named the site Mile Oak Estate. Built in the 1930s they named all the estate roads after Derby winners - Reynoldstown Lane, Bahram Road, Brown Jack Avenue, Sunstar Lane, Gainsborough Lane and Hyperion Avenue, alas these horses were not trained there. The developers name is largely forgotten and the name Stud Farm Estate remains. Known locally as the green-tiled estate as paintwork and roof tiles were green. Originally properties cost from £680 and featured all electric heating.
Since 1942 the Stud Farm Allotment and Garden Society have held their annual social and display at The Lawns, Hyperion Avenue, location that had been allocated as their tennis courts plot.

VICTORIA ROAD.
Part of the original village road structure plan. Start of Nelson Terrace were built pre 1900 as brickyard workers cottages and so-named after they visited London and saw Nelson's column. Now numbered as 25-47 Hailsham Road.
Plots 25-31 were earmarked to become a public house on a corner plot 108, and became 8 Nelson Terrace.

United Reformed Church Hall, corner of Cross Street. This building developed from a meeting in mid 1903 following donations towards the Victoria Memorial Church Room initiated at St John's Church. There had for many years been a Reading and Recreation Room in the village, although it had by then closed. Funds from an appeal went towards a freehold site at the corner of Cross Street and Victoria Road to create a combined Church Room and Men's Institute. With the passage of time a new Church Hall was erected alongside St John's Church in 1960 and the Victoria Road premises passed to the United Reformed Church for community usages.

ROYAL BRITISH LEGION, 1935-2004. Formed on May 15th 1930 they are hoping to hold a 75th Year Commemoration Service near that date in 2005. Their first premises were a 1940s Nissen hut.

55. ST LEONARDS NURSERIES, 1965. VICTORIA NURSERY, nurserymen, proprietor Ben Woods, 1955.

57. HAVELOCK HOUSE CONVALESCENT HOME, Mrs & Mrs Dhunnoo, 2004. Mrs J. White, 1965-1967. HARRY VINE, builder, 1955.

65. Harold Shaw, physician and surgery, Merville, 1955. VICTORIA HAND LAUNDRY, proprietor A.M. Cracknell, 1914.

67. Private abode built in 1947 by Shirley and Donald Harmer on land previously belonging to No 65 (Victoria Laundry). No 67 was acquired by Karen and Michael Clarke, 1985-2004.

84. QUEENSMEAD RESIDENTIAL HOME, 1987-2004, site of former Cypressus Nurseries.

WALNUT WALK

The William Daly Centre opened July 1982 and is located off St John's Road.

The resource unit was set up by Wealden District Council, Eastbourne Health Authority and ESCC Social Services Department. Today it is a registered charity and administered by the Friends of the William Daly Centre. The target being to help everyone work together to improve the quality of life for older members of the community in and around Polegate. Initial groups offering facilities from the centre included an Advice Centre, Living Memories social gatherings, Nail Cutting Service, Coffee Mornings and a Senile Dementia Support Group. Other groups covered Bridge Class, Slimming Club, Trefoil Guild, Friday Friends, Healthy Eating, Boarding-Out Landladies, Volunteer Contacts, Red Cross Aid, a Chess Club, Friendship Circle and Professional Umbrella Group.

WANNOCK ROAD.

1. NATHANIEL TANNER, wood merchant, 1 Woodlands Cottages, 1955.

WESTERN AVENUE
Southlands Estate as developed by Revell Estates in the 1930s. Builder named Davis is said to have fled to South Africa.

4. BERNARD BALDWIN, general stores, 1935.

5. Now a private house named appropriately Bon Bon. F.H. TAGG, confectioner, 1967-1986. L. MOON, confectionery and tobacconist, 1959. Mrs A.R. WATKINS, confectioner, 1946.

7. B.J. DAWSON, grocer, 1959. E.M. DAWSON, Spirella coursetiere, 1959.

WINDSOR WAY. Built by Bill Twine. from mid 1960s
56. V.A.C. DISCOUNT, and M.&.E. BUILDING SERVICES, 2004. MILLFIELDS BAKERY, 1973. N.S. COOPER, newsagents and confectionery, 1968.

58. THE CUCKOO CAFE. From Late October 2004, Jason Baldock and Scott Floathain. Previously REGENCY HOUSE INTERIORS. B. & P. SCRASE, newsagents, confectionery. 1973. N.S. COOPER, newsagents, 1960.

60. SOUTHERN PERFORMANCE CENTRE, sports car components, 2004. WINDSOR WAY NEWS, 1996. WINDSOR WAY NEWS, Sarah and Dave Burrows, 1982-1992. WINDSOR STORES, new owners October 1986. New owners also February 1984. WINDSOR STORES, groceries, 1972-1981.

62. ALISON'S, unisex hairdressers, 2004. ASTORS, hairdresser, 1996-2003. WINDSOR HARDWARE, garden supplies. cycle parts, timber and electrical supplies, 1981-1986. FAIRWAYS, hardware dealers, 1973). D-I-Y, gardening etc, 1970.

64. MILLFIELDS BAKERY, 1968-1972.

POLEGATE LIBRARY. Opened October 12th 1968. Major re-fit completed March 2001 after being closed for one month.

Ends as at 12.11.04

ACKNOWLEDGMENTS

Penny Barnes, Tony Boniface, Annette Buckley, Maureen Copping, Robert Girling, Vera Hodsoll, Ron Levett, Roy Martin, Roger Matthews and Keith Walton.

The family of Harry Hurdle, T.R. Beckett Ltd, East Sussex Record Office, Polegate Library, Sussex Express & County Herald.

TALEPIECE

Retailers like Montague Stores in Hailsham Road (now Dove brides dress hire) were once the hub of the community. Below: Perhaps this is the best way to spend the day, the site of the ancient Liberty Stone. Right: Poor old Red Croft is seen about to succumb to a demolition crew.

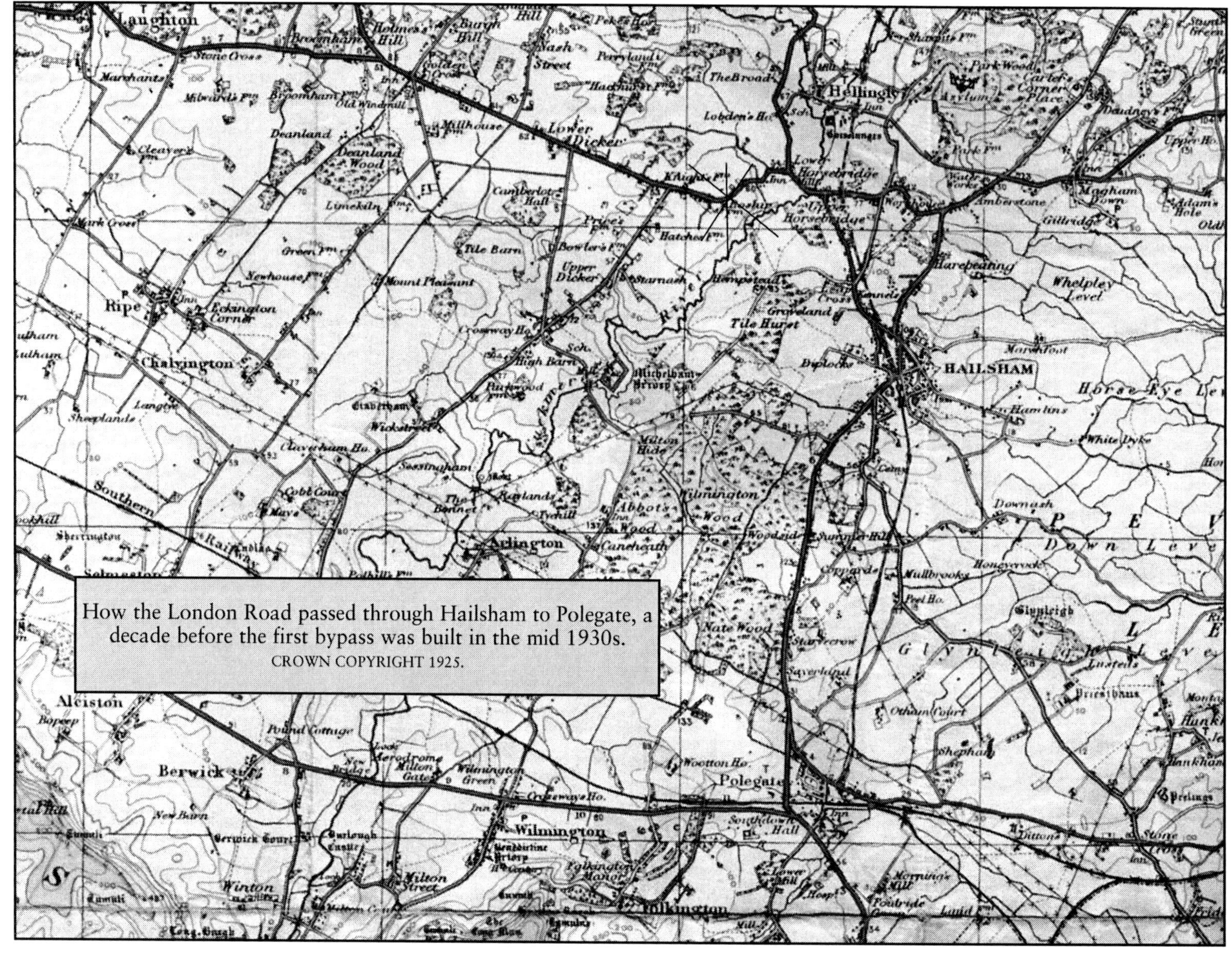

How the London Road passed through Hailsham to Polegate, a decade before the first bypass was built in the mid 1930s.
CROWN COPYRIGHT 1925.

RESEARCH AND REGENERATION
BY PETER LONGSTAFF-TYRRELL

That Peace in Our Time
The artefacts of WWII in Sussex
ISBN 0-952197-0-1 (1993)

Operation Cuckmere Haven
Military aspects of the Cuckmere Valley
ISBN 0-9521297-1-X (1997)

A Sussex Sunset
RAF Pevensey & RAF Wartling Radar, 1938-1964
ISBN 0-9521297-2-8 (1998)

Tyrrell's List
The artefacts of Two Great Wars in Sussex
ISBN 0-9521297-3-6 (1999)

Destination Fowington
East Sussex military airfields & Allied aircraft incidents
ISBN 0-9521297-4-4 (1999)

Front-Line Sussex
Napoleon Bonaparte to the Cold War
ISBN 0-7509-2592-2 (2000)

The Seaford Mutiny of 1795
The Royal Oxfordshire Militia rebellion
ISBN 0-9521297-6-0 (2000)

Tunbridge Wells to Toronto
Charlie Jenkins 1907 Diary
Possingworth Press, private edition (2001)

Barracks to Bunkers
250 years of military activity in Sussex
ISBN 0-7509-2908-1 (2002)

The Maple Leaf Army in Britain
The Canadian Army in Britain
ISBN 0-9521297-7-9 (2003)

Reflections from the Cuckmere Valley
250 years of industry and intrigue
ISBN 0-9521297-8-7 (2004)

A Picture of Polegate
Historical Notes - Picture Legacy- Urban Archive.
ISBN 0-9521297-9-5 (2004)

INDEX to sections One and Two

not including the Urban Archive which is alphabetical.

ADDITIONS

ADDITIONS